RAND

T0154932

The Value of Family Planning Programs in Developing Countries

Rodolfo A. Bulatao

Supported by the
William and Flora Hewlett Foundation
Rockefeller Foundation
United Nations Population Fund

POPULATION MATTERS

A RAND Program of Policy-Relevant Research Communication

Over the past 10 years, demographic research has produced important scientific findings on social issues of global importance, such as meeting the demand for contraception, managing immigration, reducing poverty, and anticipating the consequences of population aging. Regrettably, this research is rarely noticed by or accessible to policymakers, the media, and the general public when relevant policy deliberations occur. Frequently, the research is addressed only to scholarly audiences, and researchers seldom explain the implications of their work for policy development and implementation. All too often, the results are missed opportunities to inform policy debates with scientific information.

As a step toward addressing this problem, RAND has begun *Population Matters*, a program to synthesize and communicate the policy-relevant results of demographic research. Using a variety of approaches and formats, the program is attempting to reach audiences that make and influence population policy in the United States and abroad. The products will attempt to balance scientific rigor with accessibility.

The first issue we chose to examine was family planning in developing countries. Family planning programs have been in place for more than 30 years in many regions of the world. In the industrial nations whose donations and technical assistance support these programs, they have been relatively noncontroversial and have enjoyed broad political support throughout most of their history. However, in recent years, donor-nation support has shown signs of weakening. In the United States, traditionally the leading supporter of these programs, sharp ideological debates have surrounded the subject, and Congress has reduced program funding.

Among the issues that *Population Matters* has chosen to study, family planning is somewhat unusual in that there is a substantial amount of research and factual information on the subject that is specifically addressed to policymakers. However, much of the existing material is likely to be viewed skeptically by policy audiences. Much of it is associated with advocacy groups or an ideological point of view and thus is prone to be perceived as yet another partisan contribution to the debate rather than objective information. Our aim in producing this synthesis of the relevant research was to provide an objective and balanced account of what these programs have accomplished, whether they are still needed, and why donor nations, especially the United States, should care. We hope that the report will help provide a more scientific basis for debating the merits of family planning programs.

This report was produced with financial assistance from the William and Flora Hewlett Foundation, the Rockefeller Foundation, and the United Nations Population Fund. It should be of interest to policy audiences and general readers interested in demographic and population issues.

The *Population Matters* project is being conducted within RAND's Labor and Population Program.

For further information on the Population Matters project, contact

Julie DaVanzo, Director
Population Matters
RAND
P.O. Box 2138
1700 Santa Monica, CA 90407-1238
Email: Julie_DaVanzo@rand.org

or visit our homepage at

http://www.rand.org/popmatters

CONTENTS

FIGURES

TABLES

This report synthesizes research on family planning programs in developing countries. It focuses on what is known on three principal issues:

- The implications for developing countries of high fertility rates and unmet need for contraception
- The benefits of family planning programs
- Program costs and the role of donor nations.

The report concludes that family planning programs are providing women in developing countries with desired access to contraceptive services and helping to reduce fertility rates. These programs are also associated with a range of other benefits, most notably improvements in women's and children's health. Host countries provide about 60 to 75 percent of funding for family planning. However, funding and technical assistance from donor nations, especially the United States, have been crucial to the past success of family planning programs and are equally important for strengthening and expanding program efforts to meet future challenges.

HIGH FERTILITY AND UNMET NEED

The world's population is still growing. Although fertility has fallen worldwide from about five children per couple to about three since 1960, annual population growth in the 1990s is still approximately 80

---

[1]Prepared by RAND staff.

million people, equivalent to adding a country the size of Germany to the world's population each year. Most of this growth is occurring in developing nations, where fertility rates remain high. Sub-Saharan Africa in particular has experienced little change in its high fertility rates. Over two dozen countries have fertility rates over 6.0, notwithstanding decreases in a few countries, such as Kenya and Zimbabwe.

Even in countries where family size has approached "replacement level"— two children per couple—the population may continue to grow. This phenomenon, known as "population momentum," occurs because of the population's age structure: When a large proportion of women are in their childbearing years, the population can increase even though the rate of childbearing per woman is falling. Over the next few decades, this momentum will account for a substantial share of the world's population growth.

High fertility and rapid population growth can pose problems for developing nations. They can deny opportunities for socioeconomic development; contribute to high levels of infant mortality; and strain public resources for health, education, and other vital services.

In addition, high fertility runs counter to the preferences expressed by millions of couples in developing countries, who actually want to have smaller families. Motivated by practical concerns about finances, health, and their families' futures, millions around the world would prefer to have fewer children than they are actually having.

This gap between preferences and fertility springs from what demographers label the "unmet need for contraception." This concept refers to the needs of women who want no more children but do not practice contraception. Survey research indicates that unmet need affects an estimated 10 to 40 percent of married women of reproductive age in developing countries. Levels of unmet need are high in high-fertility countries, such as Malawi (36 percent), and can also be sizable in more developed regions, such as Latin America, where they range from 12 to 29 percent. For all developing countries, the total number of women with unmet need is estimated at 150 million.

BENEFITS OF FAMILY PLANNING

Family planning programs help developing countries address these issues. They help to moderate high fertility, fill the unmet need for contraception, and reduce the number of unwanted pregnancies. At their most elemental, family planning programs are organized efforts to provide contraception—ranging from temporary methods, such as oral contraceptives and condoms, to sterilization—and related reproductive health services. Since the first national programs in developing countries were established in the late 1950s, family planning has been associated with notable increases in the use of contraception in the developing world. This has been true across an astonishing range of cultural, political, and socioeconomic environments.

Family planning has been successful in filling unmet need by helping women in developing countries overcome obstacles to the use of contraception. The two barriers women most commonly cite are (1) lack of knowledge about contraceptive methods and availability and (2) concern about health effects. By increasing access to contraception and promoting wider knowledge about proper use and low health risks, family planning programs have helped address these barriers as well as others, such as the supply and cost of contraceptives. Reducing unmet need can also help to reduce the number of unplanned and unwanted pregnancies. Since they are more likely to end in abortion, these pregnancies increase health risks for mothers when the abortions are unsafe. Unplanned children may have other negative impacts: Families with unwanted children tend to invest less in each child's education.

However, the success of family planning programs has not been uniform. Their effectiveness has depended on several factors, including a favorable political climate, a well-structured program offering a variety of contraceptive methods, flexibility in adapting to local conditions, and stable funding sources. Nonetheless, there are success stories on all continents. Researchers and program personnel have learned a great deal—in part through work supported by the U.S. government—about how to design and operate successful programs, even in what appear to be unfavorable social and cultural environments.

Increased use of contraception has been instrumental in reducing fertility rates since the mid-1960s from about six children per couple in developing countries to about three during this interval. Statistical analysis indicates that family planning programs have been responsible for as much as 40 percent of this decline.

Lower fertility from increased use of contraception has in turn been associated with a range of benefits for developing countries. At the macroeconomic level, reduced fertility has helped create favorable conditions for socioeconomic development in some countries. A prime example of this connection has been the so-called "Asian Economic Miracle." From 1960 to 1990, the five fastest-growing economies in the world were in East Asia: South Korea, Singapore, Hong Kong, Taiwan, and Japan. Two other Southeast Asian nations, Indonesia and Thailand, were not far behind. During this 30-year span, women in East Asia reduced their childbearing from an average of six children or more to two or fewer in the span of a single generation. This reduction in fertility contributed to East Asia's remarkable socioeconomic development.

One way in which lower fertility can help promote socioeconomic development is by reducing the proportion of dependent children in the population. A lower ratio of children to adults can create what demographers call a "demographic bonus": With fewer children, families can save more or invest more money per child in, for example, education or health care. Furthermore, a smaller proportion of children means that a greater percentage of the population is in the working ages. The impressive rise in East Asian savings and investment rates since the late 1960s can be explained in part by the equally impressive decline in youth dependency burdens.

However, some caution is required in drawing connections between lower fertility and socioeconomic development. The "demographic bonus" is not automatic but contingent on appropriate policy in other areas. Furthermore, the savings from the "bonus" must be handled wisely or the effects may be negative. For example, the substantial liquidity created by savings in the East Asian countries may actually have contributed to the financial excesses that led to the Asian currency crisis of 1997.

In addition to moderating fertility, family planning can yield other benefits, including improved health for women and children and a greater degree of freedom for women. The clearest health benefit for women is reduced risk of maternal death. Death in childbirth is almost 20 times as likely for each birth in developing countries as in developed countries. Having many successive pregnancies puts mothers at even greater risk. For example, at the total fertility rate in sub-Saharan Africa of 5.6 children, the average woman has a 1 in 18 lifetime risk of dying in childbirth. Reducing fertility by half would also reduce this risk by about half. Also, lower fertility, especially at younger and older ages, and greater spacing between births reduces the risk of infant and child mortality.

Reduced dependency burdens can also improve educational performance. Countries can send more children to school and invest more per child, thus improving the quality of the future labor force. South Korea, for example, raised net secondary enrollment from 38 percent to 84 percent between 1970 and 1990, while more than tripling per-pupil expenditure. During this time, fertility declined from 4.5 births per woman to less than two. At the same time, families can invest more time and resources in educating each child.

Additional opportunities created by lower fertility include reduced pressures on public funds and a grace period for dealing with environmental pressures and for managing typically limited resources, such as water.

PROGRAM COSTS AND THE ROLE OF DONOR SUPPORT

Expenditures on family planning across all developing countries are approximately US$10 billion annually. Most of this amount is paid by national governments or individual households. Equivalent to around US$1–2 per person per year, this is not large by many standards.

Governments typically cover the bulk of family planning expenditures in developing countries. The proportion of costs they cover tends to rise as programs develop: from under 30 percent to over 60 percent of funding during the 1980s in Tunisia, for instance. In addition, funds from industrial-country development assistance, international agencies, and private sources fill critical gaps, and households also pick up some proportion of the costs, by some estimates about as much as donors do.

Funds from international donors cover a fourth to a third of public spending on family planning throughout the developing world. Per capita, developing countries receive approximately 15 cents from international donors for population and reproductive health programs. Sub-Saharan Africa, with its newer programs, receives more—over 50 percent of the total spent in the world in 1995. Asia, by contrast, with its more developed programs, receives about 10 percent. International donors play an especially prominent role in helping programs get started and later helping them expand. Typically, donor involvement decreases over time as programs mature and recipient nations become more self-sufficient in funding and operating them.

Donor commitments have fluctuated in recent years. They increased substantially, to US$1.37 billion, the year following the 1994 International Conference on Population and Development held in Cairo (as they did after the previous world conference in 1984). However, these comparisons are complicated by the expanded mandate from the Cairo conference to tackle reproductive health. Excluding funding for reproductive health, donor commitments actually fell from 1994 to 1995 by 7 percent in real terms. Even counting reproductive health funding, larger increases will be needed to meet the Cairo conference goal of donor support for a third of the cost of population and reproductive health programs by 2000.

The primary donor countries are the United States, Japan, and the other member nations of the Organisation for Economic Co-Operation and Development. Historically, the United States has been the largest contributor to population programs around the world and the most significant provider of technical assistance. However, there are signs that the United States has started to relinquish its role as world leader. The U.S. share of contributions diminished in the late 1980s and has not recovered to previous levels. In fact, U.S. population assistance fell 20 percent from fiscal 1995 to fiscal 1996 and fell a further 10 percent to fiscal 1997. The effect of these declines is uncertain. It is unclear whether other donor nations are willing or able to make up the shortfall.

THE CHALLENGES AHEAD

Despite their history of success, family planning programs still have much to accomplish. Programs face challenges in improving service, dealing with sexually transmitted diseases, including HIV/AIDS, and ensuring broader attention to women's reproductive health needs, as urged by the Cairo conference. One specific challenge will be serving the needs of the huge cohort of young women just coming to childbearing age. The group aged 15 to 24 will total 900 million by the turn of the century. Programs increasingly recognize the need for new strategies to reach these young adults. Much of the need for contraception among young adults is for delaying or spacing births. With the realization that delaying births can help reduce population momentum, programs need to revisit their goals and promotional approaches.

Another critical need is further research to improve contraceptive methods and develop new ones. Advances in this area could promote increased contraceptive use and reduce contraceptive failures, which in turn could reduce abortions, which are sometimes a consequence of such failure.

Dealing with these issues will involve building on the past success of family planning programs and strengthening current efforts with continuing support from donor nations and the international community.

ACKNOWLEDGMENTS

Useful material for this paper was provided especially by Stan Bernstein and Andrew Mason. Comments on drafts came, formally or informally, from David Adamson, Stan Bernstein, John Bongaarts, Barbara Crane, Julie DaVanzo, John Haaga, Lynn Karoly, Linda Martin, Mark Montgomery, Sally Patterson, Sara Seims, J. Joseph Speidel, Ellen Starbird, and Amy Ong Tsui and have been taken into account to the extent possible. The summary was drafted by David Adamson, RAND communications analyst. Editorial assistance was provided by Phyllis Gilmore. The paper was prepared under contract with RAND and supported by grants to RAND from the Hewlett Foundation, the Rockefeller Foundation, and UNFPA.

Chapter One

INTRODUCTION

When the Marshall Plan began after World War II, the economically prostrated countries of Western Europe had 14 percent of the world's population. Today these countries have grown rich and, with their trade and mutual cooperation in many areas, provide a bulwark to American prosperity. But they are also a smaller part of the world than they used to be, with only half their previous share of the world's population. While the industrial countries were rebuilding their economies and achieving previously unattainable levels of prosperity, the rest of the world was setting its own records, with population growth rates exceeding 1.9 percent annually over the entire period. Population outside the advanced industrial countries has almost tripled in the past 50 years.[1]

This rapid population growth is not over, despite recent reports of lower fertility[2] around the world. The first part of this report will argue that population growth persists and that family planning programs continue to be needed to moderate future growth. This argument involves several steps, to show (a) that the "population explosion" is not a "one-shot wonder" but is likely to be a nagging concern into the next century, (b) that rapid population growth because of high fertility robs countries of valuable opportunities for economic development, and (c) that high fertility is actually contrary to the

---

[1]Unless otherwise indicated, historical demographic statistics are from United Nations (1996), and population projections use the World Bank (1997a) model.

[2]For the purposes of this discussion, we follow the usage of demographers who define *fertility* as actual childbearing and *fecundity* as the potential to have children (the opposite of sterility). French demographers reverse these terms.

preferences of many people, who would prefer smaller families but, because of ignorance and sometimes unfounded fears about health effects, do nothing to restrict births.

To show how family planning programs have made and could continue to make a difference, the middle part of this report will discuss their record.   These programs are an unusual social invention, blending frank talk about previously taboo topics, large cadres of trained health workers, attractive advertising, and a strong concern with enhancing voluntary decisions and expanding women's options. Their value, if they are run properly, is demonstrated in studies ranging from the experimental to the cross-national. This contribution does not depend on a favorable socioeconomic and cultural environment, which is neither indispensable for success nor a guarantee of it. Rather, the contribution depends on how effectively a program exploits the opportunities in its environment and how it attends to the basics of service delivery.

Since no intervention is without cost, the last part of the report examines this issue. What programs cost is "pennies a day," as one report has been titled.[3] Given their wide benefits for the population, even beyond those the clients themselves receive, these programs deserve government support. Donor support, provided in the past on humanitarian grounds and to promote global prosperity, is crucial and needs to be maintained.

---

[3]Family Health International (1990).

Chapter Two

THE NEED FOR FAMILY PLANNING

POPULATION GROWTH

Over the past 50 years, the developing countries (as conventionally defined by the United Nations) added 3.2 billion people to the world's population, which has now reached 6.0 billion. Over the next 50 years, if current moderate projections hold, this same group of countries will add another 3.1 billion people to the world's population. Substantial population growth does not seem to have gone away.

Fifty years is a long period for a projection. However, shorter projections show the same trends. From 1975 to 2000, developing-country populations will have grown by 1.9 billion people (reaching 4.9 billion). From 2000 to 2025, they will continue to grow by an additional 1.8 billion people. Figure 1 shows population growth by decade in the industrial and developing countries. The peak decade for population growth in developing countries is the 1990s. Even if, as projected, growth falls off a little, it will still be well over 700 million per decade over the next 20 years, and then will decline only gradually. Industrial countries, on the other hand, will contribute little to world population growth and could as a whole experience negative growth toward the middle of the next century.

Projections naturally involve some uncertainty but are not pure speculation. After all, of the population in the year 2025, more than half have already been born, and of the population a decade from now, at least 80 percent are already among us. Historical experience

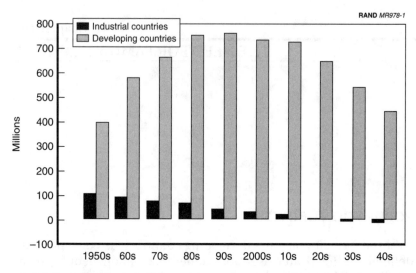

SOURCE: United Nations (1996) and projections using the World Bank (1997a) model.

**Figure 1—Population Increments by Decade in Industrial
and Developing Countries (millions)**

with patterns of childbearing can be applied to estimate the remaining proportions.[1]

The projections show continued substantial growth despite the fact that fertility has moderated in developing countries. In the 1950s, total fertility was estimated at 6.0 children per woman. By the first half of the 1990s, it had fallen almost by half, to 3.3 children per woman. Annual population growth, about 2.1 percent a year in the 1950s, is below 1.8 percent and falling.

Despite these fertility declines and even assuming they will continue, the annual increments to developing-country populations will still be large. While fertility has fallen overall, very high fertility persists in many countries: Total fertility in Uganda, for instance, has been estimated recently at 6.9 children per woman, and it is only one of

---

[1]Such projections almost always assume that current attempts to reduce the rate of population growth will continue and will not be weakened. If, instead, fertility were to cease to decline, the developing-country population would grow by 2.4 billion, not 1.8 billion, in 2000 to 2025, and by 5.8 billion, not 3.1 billion, in 2000 to 2050.

about two dozen countries with fertility at 6.0 or higher. About another two dozen countries have fertility between 5.0 and 5.9 (World Bank, 1997a). In addition, annual increments are large because developing-country populations are much bigger now and are predominantly young, with a median age of about 23. Young populations include many potential childbearers, whose children in turn will continue to swell the population. As a result, the number of babies born in developing countries should keep increasing for another two decades. The population growth rate will moderate during this period only because, as the population ages, the number of deaths will also go up.

If each couple were to have no more children than those necessary to replace themselves, developing-country populations would still continue to grow because of their young age structures. This is illustrated in Figure 2 with population pyramids, which show the distribution of population by age and sex. Each cohort (each group of people born in contiguous years) moves upward in the pyramid as it ages, and the upper levels of the pyramid therefore expand over time, as the contrast between 1995 and 2025 shows. Even if each cohort only reproduces itself (so that the lowest rung of the pyramid resembles the preceding ones), population will still grow, especially at older ages. This phenomenon, known as population momentum, will account for almost three-quarters of the population growth in developing countries over the next 25 years and for practically all the growth in East Asia. Momentum is largely absent, by contrast, in the pyramid for industrial countries (the last pyramid), which has a narrow base.[2]

---

[2]Momentum can also be compared to the long-term interest on the national debt, continuing almost indefinitely into the future. The debt exists because of a previous excess of government expenses over revenue. Momentum exists because of a previous societal "excess" of births over deaths. The quicker a balanced budget is reached, the smaller the long-term debt. Similarly, the quicker a balance of fertility and mortality is reached, the smaller the long-term population momentum. If a balanced budget cannot be reached this year, reducing the deficit will at least slow the growth in the national debt. Likewise, reducing fertility will at least slow the increase in population momentum. Even if the government achieves a balanced budget, and keeps it balanced indefinitely, interest charges will continue on the accumulated debt. Even if fertility stays at replacement level indefinitely, population will continue to grow because of the accumulated momentum. Finally, just as only applying a government budget surplus to the principal on the national debt will reduce future interest payments, only fertility below replacement will reduce future population momentum.

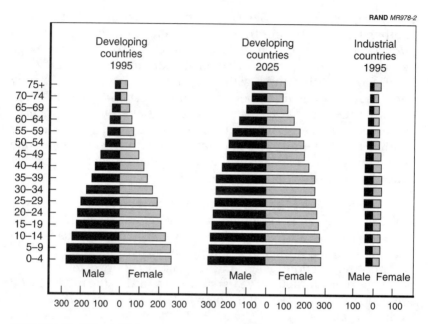

SOURCE: World Bank (1997a, 1997b) and projections using the model used there.

**Figure 2—Population Pyramids: Distribution of Population
by Age and Sex (millions)**

Continued substantial population growth can be expected in every developing-country region. Of the 1.8 billion additional people that can be expected in the next 25 years, East and Southeast Asia and the Pacific will contribute about 400 million (Figure 3). More will come from sub-Saharan Africa (almost 500 million) and South Asia (480 million). The increments will be smaller, but still substantial, in the Middle East crescent (260 million for this band of mostly Islamic countries stretching from Morocco to Kazakhstan) and in Latin America and the Caribbean (170 million). Although population growth will be most impressive in sub-Saharan Africa—leading to a population 75-percent larger by 2025 than it is today—other regions will also show impressive expansion. Latin America, for instance, will have 33 percent more people by 2025, and much of the increase will undoubtedly go to expand such already massive urban agglomerations as Mexico City.

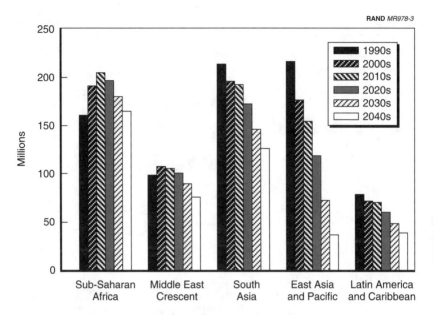

SOURCE: Estimated using the World Bank (1997a) projection model.

Figure 3—Population Increments by Decade in Developing-
Country Regions (millions)

IMPLICATIONS OF HIGH FERTILITY

Expanding megacities will be among the substantial changes that
these large population increments will bring. Countrysides will
probably be more densely settled, and infrastructure and human
services will be either substantially more extensive or under greater
stress. The half century of growth since World War II has, for example, seen the Philippines increase from 70 to 226 people per square
kilometer of land, and Bangladesh from 290 to 821 people per square
kilometer. (At the latter density, the United States would have 7.7
billion people, not 270 million.)

Contrasts between the rapidly expanding developing countries and
the steadily growing industrial economies can be extreme. Figure 4,
for instance, compares income levels (gross national product, or

GNP, per capita), the labor force in agriculture, and infant mortality.[3] Average income in developing countries is less than one-twentieth of that in industrial countries. The proportion of the labor force in agriculture is on average more than 10 times as large as in indus-

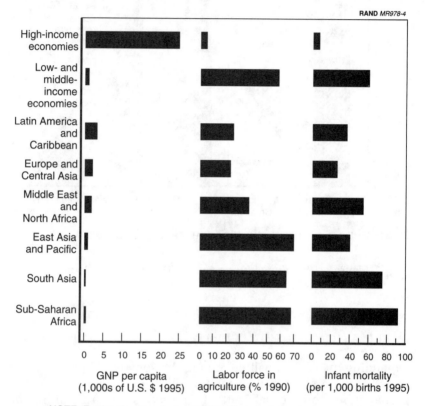

NOTE: Regional averages are weighted by population (or by number of births, for infant mortality) and exclude high-income economies. Data from World Bank (1997b).

Figure 4—Indicators for High-Income Economies and Low-and Middle-Income Regions

[3]The groups compared, strictly speaking, are high-income economies versus low- and middle-income economies, as defined in World Bank (1997b). "Europe and Central Asia" includes only the low- and middle-income economies in that region.

trial countries. And babies in developing countries die at a rate more than eight times that of industrial countries, producing average life expectancies about a dozen years shorter.

How much of the difference in development and human welfare is explained by rapid population growth? A number of previous studies have produced inconclusive and even conflicting results. Cross-national regression analyses with data from the 1970s suggested that population growth did not affect national income, but studies of the 1980s suggested a negative impact.[4] Population growth, after all, provides not only more consumers of societal resources and services but also more workers and producers of goods, a greater pool of human resources for developing new products and technology. The relevance of expanded pools of consumers and producers may depend on economic and social policies that are often enacted with little attention to population. The net effect of population on development could therefore vary across countries and periods and could be difficult to assess.

What is clear, however, is that different sources of population growth have different economic implications. A population growing through migration often puts the migrants to work, earning some return from their labor.[5] A population growing because of substantially longer life expectancies could in principle keep older people working longer to prevent any increase in dependency, although societal preferences and practices may preclude this. But a population growing because of high fertility must accept that those added to the population will spend years as dependents, becoming socialized and educated, before they are productive.

Dependency and Savings

The South Korean experience can illustrate how high fertility contributes to large numbers of dependents. Total fertility was well above four children per woman until 1970, and for every 100 persons

---

[4]See Ahlburg (1996) for a recent review of this general area.

[5]Smith and Edmonston (1997) conclude, for instance, that U.S. residents gain economically from the presence of immigrants because of the additional labor (generally remunerated at lower rates than the average) and the increased specialization.

of working age (15–64) there were between 70 and 90 dependents (either younger or older). But fertility was declining rapidly, and the dependency ratio followed it down, so that now there are only 40 dependents per 100 persons of working age, fewer than the 50 per 100 typical in other industrial countries (Figure 5). The dependency ratio will rise again in the future as the population ages, but since the mid-1980s, South Korea has enjoyed a relatively light dependency burden and will for several more decades.

A key argument in a landmark study 40 years ago was that a light dependency burden should be good for economic growth (Coale and Hoover, 1958). Among the effects of the dependency burden, the way it depresses savings has recently received renewed attention. Arguments about this have gone back and forth among economists, but improved models now confirm this effect cross-nationally (Kelley and Schmidt, 1996). An analysis of household income and expenditures in Great Britain, Taiwan, Thailand, and the United States concludes that "in all countries except Thailand, more children depress

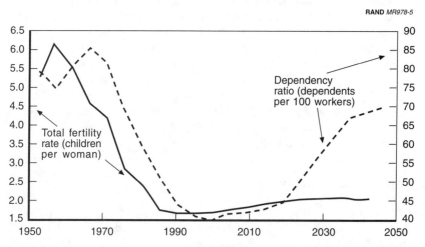

SOURCE: United Nations (1996) and World Bank (1997a).

Figure 5—Total Fertility Rate and Dependency Ratio,
South Korea, 1950–2050

the saving rate" (Deaton and Paxson, 1997, p. 106).[6] Careful analysis of the experience of East Asian countries suggests that their reductions in fertility in the past decades relieved not only dependency burdens but also dependence on foreign capital by contributing to high saving rates (Higgins and Williamson, 1997; Williamson and Higgins, 1997; Lee et al., 1997; Bloom and Williamson, 1997).

Saving rates are indeed exceptionally high in East Asia: 35 percent of gross domestic product (GDP) in Northeast Asia and 33 percent in Southeast Asia, in contrast to 21 percent in the countries of the Organization for Economic Cooperation and Development (OECD) and only 10 percent in South Asia.[7] Relying less on government services, the multitude of households save substantial amounts as their members save to provide for retirement; possibly to fund bequests to the next generation; sometimes to hedge against financial setbacks; and occasionally to anticipate large expenditures, such as those for children's education. Over their lives, people ordinarily save most in their middle years when they are most productive, provided their child-rearing expenses have declined. And as life expectancies rise, Asian workers, increasingly less confident of being able to depend on children in old age and unprotected by elaborate social security schemes, have also been pressed to save more for retirement.

Figures 6 and 7 show trends in dependency ratios, savings, and investment in Northeast and Southeast Asia.[8] As expected, savings

---

[6]However, Deaton and Paxson go on to try to estimate the aggregate effect of population growth on the saving rate and find it is trivial (and actually has the reverse sign). They achieve this contradictory result with a model that assumes a stable population (contrary to the typical situation in a developing country, in which life expectancies are rising and fertility is falling) and unchanging age profiles of income and saving (contrary to their own empirical findings). These unusual assumptions may be largely responsible for their perverse aggregate results: A stable population, for instance, will have a different distribution of age groups—and therefore different proportions of high-saving and low-saving households—than a population nearing the end of fertility transition.

[7]For present purposes, Northeast Asia covers Japan, South Korea, Taiwan, Hong Kong, and Singapore; Southeast Asia covers Indonesia, Malaysia, the Philippines, and Thailand.

[8]The graphs show unweighted averages across countries, leaving out Taiwan for dependency ratios. Savings and investment rates cover five-year periods centered around the given dates, except that the last point is for 1990–1992 (Williamson and

and investment generally moved in the opposite direction from dependency, rising as lower fertility reduced the size of dependent cohorts. To determine whether this apparent link is causal requires investigating many possible complicating factors. For instance, strong economic growth itself can produce greater savings, as households find their incomes augmented by unexpected windfalls. When such relationships are accounted for, however, the results still suggest that dependency has a strong effect on savings.

For Northeast Asia, the net effect of a dependency ratio above 60 percent in the early 1970s was to depress savings by 5.2 percentage points (as a share of GDP), whereas the net effect of a dependency ratio close to 40 percent in the early 1990s was to increase savings by 8.4 percentage points (Williamson and Higgins, 1997).[9] These percentages are not trivial. For South Korea, for example, an 8.4-point increase was worth additional savings of close to US$25 billion a year in the early 1990s. This figure exceeds the total official development assistance received by all of East Asia and the Pacific in 1991 (US$17 billion) and is equal to more than half the assistance received by all developing countries combined (US$47 billion).

Net effects of dependency on investment were similar: A reduction of 3.7 percentage points in the early 1970s contrasts with an increase of 5.4 percentage points in the early 1990s. The dependency burden contributed to these countries' international debt from 1950 to 1980, but the lighter dependency burden has contributed to positive current account balances since then. A similar, but slightly more moderate, pattern of net effects on savings and investment has been demonstrated for Southeast Asia (Williamson and Higgins, 1997).

The net effect of dependency ratios was large enough to produce all the decline in foreign capital dependence after 1970 in both Northeast and Southeast Asia, by itself turning these regions from net debtors to net creditors on world capital markets. It also produced

---

Higgins, 1997). Dependency ratios are for the middle of each period (United Nations, 1996).

[9]That is, savings were depressed or increased by the amounts given relative to what they would have been if "population age shares" had been at the 1950–1992 means.

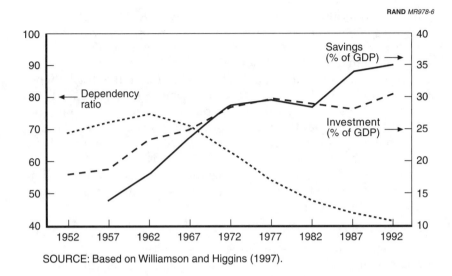

SOURCE: Based on Williamson and Higgins (1997).

Figure 6—Dependency, Savings, and Investment in Northeast Asia

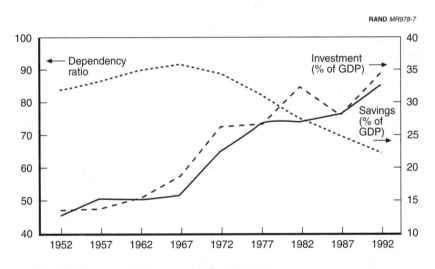

SOURCE: Based on Williamson and Higgins (1997).

Figure 7—Dependency, Savings ,and Investment in Southeast Asia

substantial capital deepening: From 1965 to 1990, capital per worker grew 2.7 percent annually in the United States, but 6.6 percent annually in Thailand, 7.6 percent in Japan, 8.6 percent in South Korea, and 8.7 percent in Taiwan (Summers et al., 1995). (Although the United States appears disadvantaged in this comparison, it actually benefited by using East Asian savings to finance its perennial trade deficit.) The substantial liquidity these savings created, plus the additional investment attracted from foreign sources, could have contributed to the financial excesses, given lack of effective bank regulation, that led to the Asian currency crisis in 1997.[10] Clearly, a savings bonus from favorable demography can cut two ways: Failing to use it productively can be, eventually, as injurious as investing it well can be beneficial.

The large effects of reduced dependency on savings owed something to the fact that these economies were rapidly growing, and the impact of dependency changes could be magnified by other factors. But this issue aside, East Asia does not appear to be a special case. Modeling suggests that the effect of a given demographic shock on the current account balance has been no different in the rest of the world. However, in such regions as South Asia, where dependency reductions have so far been smaller, the impact has been correspondingly less positive (Williamson and Higgins, 1997; Bloom and Williamson, 1997).

Education and Health

Smaller birth cohorts should reduce the pressure on schools, allowing improvements in education. Across developing countries, expenditures per pupil rise as the proportion of the population that is of school age declines. But education spending in total does not necessarily increase, and enrollment rates do not always rise (Schultz, 1987). The "demographic bonus" from declining fertility, which could be spent to increase enrollment or improve the quality

---

[10]Krugman (1998) provides an interpretation of the crisis that explains its untraditional character: Implicit government guarantees for banks and finance companies, coupled with poor regulation, led to distorted investment decisions and an eventual collapse in asset prices.

of education, is sometimes spent instead on ineffective educational systems or on other things besides education.

Where the "demographic bonus" does go to improve education, the results can be salutary. For instance, South Korea raised net secondary enrollment from 38 to 84 percent between 1970 and 1990 and more than tripled expenditure per secondary pupil (Ahlburg and Jensen, 1997).[11] Demographic factors were not the only ones at work, but for East Asia as a whole they are estimated to have contributed 3–4 percent of the rise in enrollment and 10–13 percent of the increased expenditure (Williamson and Higgins, 1997).

Lower fertility presumably is a boon not only for the educational system as a whole but also for individual parents in educating their children. With fewer children, parents should have more resources, time, and energy to spend on each child. Empirical studies generally confirm that fewer children means each gets more education, although the effect is neither universal nor necessarily sizable (see, for example, Rosenzweig and Wolpin, 1980; Knodel et al., 1990; Foster and Roy, 1993; Lloyd, 1994). One of the larger effects is for the Dominican Republic: In households that had avoided any unwanted births, 56 percent of children completed primary school, as opposed to only 39 percent of children in households with two or more unwanted births. This effect of "unwantedness" is similar, although weaker, in the Philippines but does not appear in Egypt or Kenya (Montgomery and Lloyd, 1996).[12] As with the demographic bonus at the societal level, the effect of fertility on education at the household level may depend on context. When parents see improved futures for their children with education, consider it an affordable priority, bear at least some costs of sending children to school, and have begun to plan their families with children's education in mind, lower fertility can contribute to more educated children (Lloyd, 1994).

---

[11]In the 1960–1985 period, high enrollment levels (especially at the primary level but also at the secondary level) accounted for more than twice as much economic growth in Korea as the level of investment (Page et al., 1993).

[12]Montgomery et al. (forthcoming) confirm the effect of unwantedness in further analysis but suggest it may be smaller, less than a year of schooling completed on average in the countries where it appears.

Lower fertility also produces healthier children. Closely spaced children, large numbers of children in each family, and children born to younger mothers are all more common before fertility declines, and such children all face higher mortality risks. Even up to the age of five years, the risk of death is greater if the interval since the preceding birth is shorter. The risk of death in the first month of life (the neonatal period) is 35–60 percent higher after a birth interval under 2 years than after an interval of 2–4 years (as Figure 8 shows for three regions). On the other hand, if the interval is longer than four years, the risk of neonatal death is reduced by 10 percent. Deaths in the postneonatal period (one month to one year) and in early childhood (1–4 years) show even more striking effects (Figure 8). Some of these effects of child survival may reflect limits on household resources for nutrition or health care, but physiological factors are also at work.

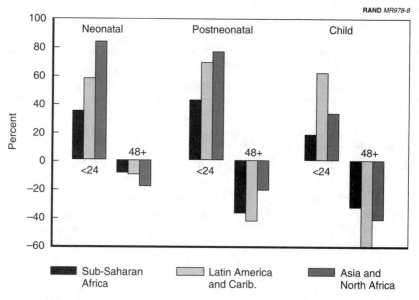

NOTE: Medians for 12 sub-Saharan, 10 Latin America, and 6 Asian–North African countries, excluding cases where the preceding sibling died before the following child's second birthday (Sullivan et al., 1994).

Figure 8—Percentage Change in Risk of Death When Preceding Birth Interval Is Shorter or Longer than 24–48 Months

Close spacing interferes with breastfeeding, which has an important role in child nutrition and in protecting the child from infection.

Child survival is also affected by birth order, although this is not evident in sub-Saharan Africa. In several countries in that region, the risk of mortality under age 5 is still as high as one in five, and the risk in the region as a whole is equally high for all children (Figure 9). But in other regions, first, second, and third children clearly benefit from lower mortality, while children beyond the sixth continue to bear substantially greater risk. The effect of the mother's age is similar: Children of older mothers (35 and older) do not seem to be at greater risk in sub-Saharan Africa because every child is at high risk, but elsewhere children of older mothers bear a 10–25 percent greater risk. Even in sub-Saharan Africa, however, children of mothers under 20 have a 20–30 percent higher risk of death than do children of older mothers.

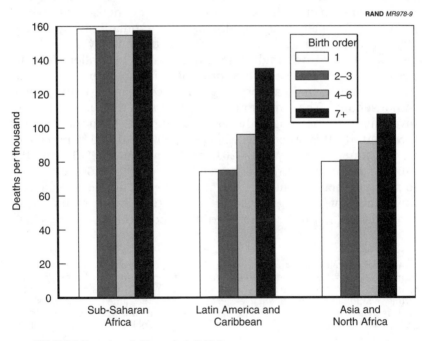

SOURCE: Based on Sullivan et al. (1994).

Figure 9—Under-Five Mortality (per thousand), by Birth Order

The mother's health also benefits from lower fertility. The clearest benefit is a reduced risk of maternal death. Death in childbirth is about 20 times as likely for each birth in developing countries as in industrial countries. Having many successive pregnancies puts a mother at even greater risk. At the total fertility rate for sub-Saharan Africa of 5.6 children, the average woman has a lifetime risk of dying in childbirth of about 1 in 18. If total fertility could be approximately halved, this lifetime risk would also be halved, to 1 in 35.[13]

The Built and Natural Environments

Although the effects of lower fertility on health may be visible fairly quickly, the effects on public investments may take longer to work themselves out. Pressures from high fertility can last for an extended period, as the housing situation in Thailand illustrates. In the early 1960s, expenditures on housing were 90 percent of what was required to keep up with the growth in number of households (which grow proportionally more rapidly than the population). By around 1980, even though fertility had declined substantially, households were still increasing rapidly, and expenditures had fallen to 50–60 percent of what was needed to prevent a decline in previous standards. Merely to maintain housing growth comparable to the growth of households, Thailand would have had to put 40 percent of all investment into housing in the 1990–1995 period. With substantially lower fertility, this proportion will fall, by 2005–2010, to 31 percent of all investment, and by 2010–2015 to 25 percent. In 15 years the number of housing starts will have to be 18 percent more numerous to maintain housing quality. But if fertility had not fallen as much, the number of housing starts would have to be even greater. In 15 years in the Philippines (where fertility is now roughly twice as high

---

[13]Maternal mortality ratios are taken from Tsui et al. (1997, p. 115) and total fertility from World Bank (1997a), adjusted upward by 20 percent to allow for pregnancies terminated without a live birth. An important assumption is that the women whose fertility would fall to bring down average fertility bear the same underlying risk per birth as those whose fertility would not fall. If those women whose fertility would fall bear a lower risk per birth—perhaps related to higher socioeconomic status, which could produce greater propensity to use contraception—the reduction in average life-time risk would be less. On the other hand, these women might bear higher risk per birth—perhaps because of a greater likelihood their pregnancies are unintended and could lead to potentially unsafe abortions—in which case the reduction in average lifetime risk would be greater.

as in Thailand), annual housing starts will have to be 53 percent more numerous (Mason, 1996).

Besides raising the need for housing, high fertility produces more mouths to be fed. The link from this to increased food production to the clearance of forests is probably the most carefully studied of the environmental threats from rapid population growth. Studies of Thailand's poorest and most populous region, the northeast, illustrate the problem. Given few job opportunities in the 1970s and 1980s and a population with little cash and no special skills, farming absorbed most of the labor. But with soil fertility low, forests had to be cleared to provide more land, and the fallow cycle became shorter and shorter. Econometric studies show that a 10-percent increase in population growth contributed to a 3.3-percent increase in deforestation (Panayotou, 1994, pp. 172–173). A broader metanalysis of quantitative studies by Palloni (1994) indicates that population growth, in association with other factors, does make a modest contribution to deforestation cross nationally.

Other aspects of the environment, from fish stocks to water supplies, may feel a similar pressure from rapid population growth. In each case, appropriate technology and institutions to control access to and use of common resources could limit environmental damage and preserve resources for the future. But lower fertility and slower population growth, it is argued, would also relieve some of the pressure on resources and allow time to develop and institute the necessary policies. Even where the contribution of population growth to an environmental problem is small—as it is, for instance, for air pollution from carbon dioxide emissions—reducing population growth may still be cost-effective, requiring proportionally less investment than various technological or other policy measures (Birdsall, 1994).[14]

Lower fertility therefore provides societies with opportunities, especially in the form of increased savings that could spur investment and economic growth, a "demographic bonus" that could be spent to improve education, and fewer high-risk births that could lead to healthier childhoods, if other health risks can be contained. Addi-

---

[14]For broad overviews of environmental and political effects, see Population Action International (1996) and Mazur (1997).

tional opportunities include reduced pressure on public expenditures and the grace period that lower fertility and slower population growth provide for dealing with pressures on the environment and for managing such typically limited resources as a society's water supplies. Seizing such opportunities could provide a political bonus to regimes that need to be increasingly concerned with the welfare of their populations and could eventually be part of the process that transforms a society into a stable and prosperous contributor to the international order. But none of this is automatic, even with substantial fertility decline. Each of the potential benefits of such a decline will only be realized with appropriate governmental policies—on investment, on education, on health, on environmental protection, and so on.

DESIRE FOR SMALLER FAMILIES

These potential benefits, however substantial they could appear to government planners, may not be the most important argument for seeking lower fertility. More significant is the fact that millions of couples in developing countries actually want to have smaller families. Motivated not by macroeconomic considerations but by practical concerns about family finances, health and well-being, and the future of their offspring, millions around the world would prefer to have fewer children than they are actually having.

Figure 10 compares the number of children women wanted, on average, in the early 1990s with total fertility across 28 developing countries in the 1990–1995 period. These countries are arrayed from those with the highest to those with the lowest desired family size. Except where desired family size exceeds six children (a setting somewhat overrepresented in this figure because more than half the data are from sub-Saharan Africa), the actual number of children tends to exceed the number desired by about three-fourths of a child on average.[15]

---

[15]Looking at number wanted person by person, one can identify births that exceed each person's desired number. Such calculations indicate even more "unwanted" births than suggested by Figure 10 (Bankole and Westoff 1995:24–25).

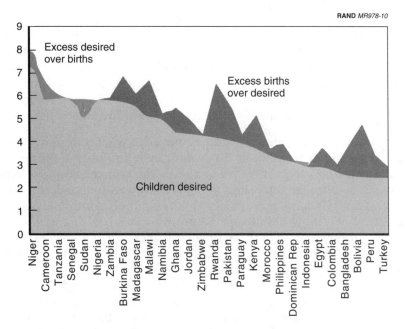

NOTE: Where available, desired family size is for all women; otherwise, it is for women ever married (Bankole and Westoff, 1995).

Figure 10—Number of Children Desired and Total Fertility in 28 Countries

These statistics refer to what women—mostly married women—want. But men tend to have fairly similar, only slightly higher, preferences, except in the highest-fertility settings. Again excepting countries where average desired family size exceeds six children, men's preferred family size is usually higher than women's by no more that 0.1 or 0.2 children (Ezeh et al., 1996, p. 29) and therefore is still most often below actual fertility.

Unmet Need

The gap between preferences and actual fertility springs from what demographers label the "unmet need for contraception." Through survey questions that identify women who would prefer to delay or terminate childbearing but who are not using contraception despite the risk of pregnancy,[16] demographers estimate that unmet need affects 10 to 40 percent of married women of reproductive age in developing countries. Levels of unmet need (Table 1) are high in high-fertility countries, such as Malawi (36 percent), but are still substantial in relatively advanced regions, such as Latin America, where they range from 12 to 29 percent. For all developing countries, the total with unmet need is estimated at about 150 million women.[17]

Unmet need is essentially a conflict between what a woman wants and what she does about it: She wants lower fertility but fails to do what is needed to prevent pregnancy. The reasons couples want smaller families are numerous and generally well-founded, from the financial strain large numbers of children put on households to the strain of continual childbearing on a woman's health and energy. Preferences for small families inevitably increase as societies modernize: Financial pressures grow; the need to educate children becomes more apparent; and the desire for more creature comforts or at least for release from unremitting childbearing begins to seem possible as the media promote alternative lifestyles. At levels of fertility reported in some earlier national surveys (as in Kenya in the 1977–1978 period), women spent the equivalent of six continuous years of their lives pregnant and 23 years caring for children younger than six years old (World Bank, 1993a, p. 9). With the early childbearing typical in some countries, pregnancy can account for more than a quarter of female school dropouts, beginning as young as primary school.[18] Controlling their fertility can give women options and a degree of freedom not previously available.

---

[16]This excludes those assumed not to be at risk: (1) those protected by postpartum anovulation, the temporary infertility that follows a pregnancy, which can be extended by continued full breastfeeding; and (2) the infecund, identified by not having conceived in five years despite taking no preventive measures, by not having menstruated in six months, or by claiming they could not have a baby or were menopausal.

[17]According to unpublished tabulations of Demographic and Health Survey data by Shea Rutstein (1997, personal communication). Precise definitions and therefore estimates of unmet need do vary somewhat, but the total of the estimates in Table 1— 75 million women with unmet need across only 44 developing countries—appears consistent with this.

[18]As in Cameroon, as reported by Eloundou-Enyegue (1997).

Table 1

Married Women of Reproductive Age with an Unmet Need for Contraception

Country	Survey Year	Percent	Number (1000s)
Africa			
Botswana	1988	27	27
Burkina Faso	1992–1993	33	522
Burundi	1987	25	201
Cameroon	1991	22	347
Ghana	1994	33	759
Kenya	1993	36	1,101
Liberia	1986	33	131
Madagascar	1992	32	551
Malawi	1992	36	498
Mali	1987	23	435
Namibia	1992	22	22
Niger	1992	19	243
Nigeria	1990	22	3,928
Rwanda	1992	37	332
Senegal	1992–1993	29	350
Sudan	1989–1990	25	940
Tanzania	1991–1992	27	1,065
Uganda	1988–1989	27	707
Zambia	1992	31	368
Zimbabwe	1994	15	207
Asia			
Bangladesh	1994	18	3,852
India	1992	20	31,005
Indonesia	1991	14	4,427
Nepal	1991	28	970
Pakistan	1991–1992	32	5,738
Philippines	1993	26	2,512
Sri Lanka	1987	12	332
Thailand	1987	11	999
Latin America and the Caribbean			
Bolivia	1994	24	235
Brazil	1986	13	3,034
Colombia	1990	12	545
Dominican Rep.	1991	17	171
Ecuador	1987	24	411
El Salvador	1985	26	182
Guatemala	1987	29	382
Mexico	1987	24	3,133

Table 1—Continued

Country	Survey Year	Percent	Number (1000s)
Paraguay	1990	15	395
Peru	1991–1992	16	471
Trinidad/Tobago	1987	16	32
Middle East Crescent			
Egypt	1992	22	1,818
Jordan	1990	22	110
Morocco	1992	20	650
Tunisia	1988	20	217
Turkey	1992	11	1,062

Source: Robey et al. (1996).

Lower fertility preferences are translated into lower fertility in the long run. Over many years, successive cohorts reduce their fertility to modern low levels in the course of socioeconomic development. But this process is lengthy and not automatic: It took a century in industrial countries and several decades in such countries as South Korea and Thailand. In the process, many couples must cope with larger families than they want and with poorly timed births.

Reasons for Unmet Need

The reasons for this delay are discernible in the obstacles women cite to contraception when they otherwise have good reason to use it. These obstacles are shown in Figure 11, which tabulates the principal reasons respondents give in surveys taken in 13 countries for not using contraception when they want to avoid a birth (Bongaarts and Bruce, 1995). These reasons are grouped for convenience into four categories: poor access, concerns about using contraception, objections to family planning, and other reasons. The most important single reason is lack of knowledge about contraception, its use, or its availability, cited by one-quarter of those with unmet need. The second most important is concern about the health effects of contraception, cited by one-fifth.

Neither obstacle is something most women in developing countries can overcome without help, and poorly educated and impoverished

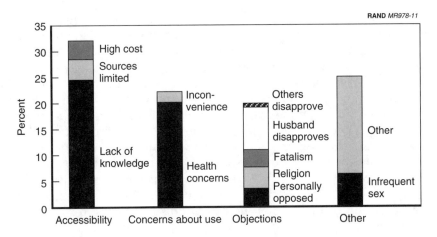

NOTE: "Sources limited" is referred to as "lack of access/difficult to get" in the original study (Bongaarts and Bruce, 1995).

Figure 11—Why Women Do Not Use Contraception Despite Wanting to Avoid a Birth (percent)

women should not need to rely entirely on the altruism of pharmaceutical firms or private doctors for education about contraception and provision of safe and appropriate methods. Contraception is in fact quite safe. What health risks some methods carry are small relative to the risks of a typical pregnancy. It is estimated that the mortality risk of an unplanned, unwanted pregnancy is 20 times the risk of any modern contraceptive method and 10 times the risk of a properly performed abortion (Ross and Frankenberg, 1993, p. 86). Still, misuse of contraceptives is possible and needs to be minimized by promoting wide knowledge of contraception and ensuring safe and effective services.

Family planning programs—organized efforts to provide contraception and provide associated reproductive health services—address the two main obstacles to contraceptive use, as well as various others, such as limits on the supply of contraceptives and their cost. The cost, to impoverished couples, can be substantial: The retail price of an annual supply of contraceptive pills exceeds US$100 in half a dozen developing countries, as does the retail price of an annual supply of condoms. Costs that reach 5 percent of average household income are common, and costs reach 20 percent of income in some sub-Saharan countries (World Bank, 1993a, pp. 33–34). Inadequate supply and high cost are each cited as the main obstacle to contraception by 3–4 percent of women, but these low figures may be misleading. For instance, someone with poor knowledge about contraceptives is unlikely to complain about supply or cost (Ross, 1995). The low salience of these reasons may also reflect program successes in supplying cheap contraceptives at the same time they raise awareness. The proportion of women with an unmet need for contraception who cite lack of knowledge as the main obstacle is sharply lower in countries where education programs are more active. The proportion citing health concerns, on the other hand, is not reduced but rises, suggesting one of the continuing challenges to such programs.[19]

The other reasons for unmet need are more problematic. Objections to family planning that the woman or others who influence her may have are fairly important, but exactly what these objections are is not clear from the survey evidence. A husband may disapprove, for instance, because he wants more children or because he is concerned about health effects, bothered by the inconvenience, or distrustful of traditional methods.[20] Such objections may therefore also reflect informational or access issues or health concerns. Except for a woman's personal opposition to contraception, the objections also appear to be less prominent where programs are active.

Family planning programs therefore appear capable of addressing the main obstacles to contraceptive use, potentially helping couples attain their desired family size and, in theory, providing societies with the demographic bonus that comes from reducing fertility. What such programs have actually contributed requires some examination.

---

[19]The correlation across 13 countries between family planning effort in 1989 and the proportion of those with unmet need citing lack of knowledge is –0.81. Using the proportion of all women rather than just those with unmet need, the correlation is –0.73. Similar correlations, for health concerns, are 0.52 and 0.09. Thus, women with health concerns increase with family planning effort as a proportion of those with unmet need, though not as a proportion of all women.

[20]An intensive study in the Philippines confirms the importance of husband's objections but does not reveal the reasons behind them (Casterline, Perez, and Biddlecom, 1997, pp. 183–184).

Chapter Three

THE RECORD OF FAMILY PLANNING

National family planning programs have been associated with notable increases in contraceptive use and consequent declines in fertility. Family planning programs predominantly emphasize voluntary acceptance of contraception, usually include an important informational and educational component, and focus especially on the needs of married women but often also reach others The "cafeteria" approach, meaning the provision of many types of contraceptives so that each person can choose the most appropriate, is often favored but often also honored in the breach. Oral contraceptives and condoms are the base of many programs' inventories, but some earlier programs relied and continue to rely heavily on methods, such as the intrauterine device (IUD), that are less prominent in programs that started later. Over time, such newer methods as injectables and implants have found their own niches. Overall, however, the main trend has been toward permanent methods: sterilization has become simpler and more demanded and now accounts for half of all contraceptive use.

How contraceptives are delivered to potential users varies. Building on efforts by private doctors and voluntary organizations, early programs (and most in their earlier phases) depended on clinics, which can offer a wide range of methods and ensure appropriate medical facilities. The limited number of clinics quickly poses a problem in a developing country; over time, various ways to bring contraceptives to people in their villages, homes, and work places have been devised. Many programs have diversified, adding such approaches as community-based distribution, mobile teams, home visiting, subsidized commercial sales, or employee programs. The clinical component in many programs receives relatively less emphasis, and program personnel have become more varied as nurses, midwives, pharmacists, and lay distributors have taken on larger roles.

Focusing primarily on contraceptive use, programs target the primary behavior change that causes fertility to decline in the transition from high, traditional, relatively stable fertility to low, modern levels at which couples are only replacing themselves. Fertility is also affected by other important behaviors (called "proximate determinants" by demographers). Of these, marriage delay in the course of modernization contributes to lower fertility, although to a lesser extent; breastfeeding tends to decline, raising fertility somewhat, because the menses return more quickly; and abortion has an important though highly variable effect. Individual programs may include interventions to affect marriage, breastfeeding, and abortion, but such interventions have tended to be limited. Nevertheless, programs have affected these other proximate determinants at least indirectly. In the long run, readily available contraception reduces resort to abortion. Trend data over 30 years for Hungary, for example, show abortion declining with increased contraceptive use, as do data from other settings, such as South Korea. Recent reports from Russia and Kazakhstan show declines in abortion in the 1990s as contraceptive services expanded.[1] However, in the early years of a program, abortion may become more common if services cannot fill the demand to limit fertility.

Experimental, country-specific, and cross-national evidence indicates that, by increasing contraceptive use, programs do contribute substantially to reducing fertility. This effect, however, is not universal. It depends on a program adopting a strategy responsive to whatever specific demand for contraception exists in the sociocultural setting, as well as on the staff mastering the basics of service delivery.

THE EFFECT OF FAMILY PLANNING PROGRAMS

National programs were established beginning in the 1950s and multiplied most rapidly from the mid-1960s to the late 1970s, when

---

[1] But even at high levels of contraceptive prevalence, abortion does not entirely disappear, partly because of contraceptive failures. The legality or illegality of abortion has little influence on such trends (Cohen, 1997).

on average five new programs were established each year. In a number of instances, national programs expanded the work done by earlier, pioneering private programs, such as those supported by the International Planned Parenthood Federation. National programs naturally required government sanction and often also enjoyed substantial support and technical assistance in many phases of their operation from international donors.

Growth in contraceptive use after programs were established is illustrated in Figure 12, showing a range of experience and some notable spurts in contraceptive use that led to declines in fertility. These examples could be multiplied: Increases in contraceptive prevalence (the proportion of married women of reproductive age using contraception) and consequent fertility declines have occurred in every region of the developing world, from Peru to Mongolia, and from Iran to South Africa. But as Figure 12 illustrates, simply starting a program does not guarantee immediate increased contraceptive use. Contraceptive use did rise quickly in South Korea, where prevalence grew close to 3 percentage points a year—sufficient to reach low,

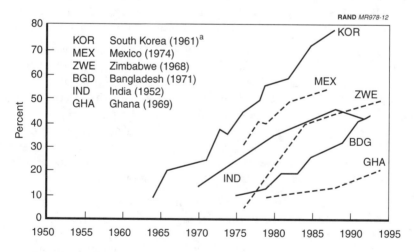

SOURCE: Based on World Bank (1993a).
[a]Dates indicate year of program start.

Figure 12—Starting Date for Family Planning Program and Contraceptive Prevalence, Selected Countries

replacement fertility within 25 years, essentially in a generation. But, in contrast, growth in contraceptive prevalence began late and proceeded haltingly in Ghana, where the increase was only 0.7 points a year. Even in such cases as South Korea, the credit that programs can fairly claim for fertility reduction has been a topic of some debate. Perhaps, some have argued, economic growth in Korea was so fast that fertility would have declined even in the absence of a program. Indeed, analysis suggests that programs cannot claim all the credit for fertility decline, but they can clearly claim some credit.

Field experiments usually indicate that well-done family planning programs are welcomed and make a difference. Researchers have looked at various elements of programs—the use of home visits, field-worker incentives, consistent supervision of field workers, pill prescription practices, postpartum education, etc.—to confirm a small but significant program effect on contraceptive acceptance or continuation (Bauman, 1994). Focusing on specific features of small-area programs, experiments can clearly demonstrate the contribution of program activities and exclude other explanations for changes in contraceptive use and fertility, in the process illustrating useful options for programs. However, such experiments do not address whether programs can have broader, nationwide effects.

This effect must be assessed against that of socioeconomic development. Improved standards of living should make contraceptives more affordable, as well as convincing many couples to opt for smaller families. Do programs then merely substitute for private provision of contraceptives—are they a natural but superfluous government response to consumer demand and consequent public pressure? Or do programs, through their promotional activities and the services they provide (much more promptly than market mechanisms would), play a leading role in reducing fertility?

Answering such questions and determining the historical contribution of large national programs is difficult. Comparisons are necessary across countries with different types of programs or with no programs. Analysts have generally relied on a reputational measure of "program effort," produced by rating 90 or so national programs with regard to the access they provide to contraceptive methods, their management effectiveness, their efforts at informing and educating people, and a number of other such dimensions, 30 in all. Analysis of program effort scores confirms that programs have been more active in more advanced developing countries. Socioeconomic development allows programs to operate more efficiently and, in leading to lower fertility preferences, to be more effective at providing contraceptive services. But relatively high levels of development, although helpful, do not appear to be essential. Bangladesh, one of the world's 20 poorest countries, has a program rated among the 10 best in the developing world and has seen a substantial decline in fertility over the last decade.

Multivariate statistical analysis suggests, in fact, that family planning programs do contribute independently to reduced fertility, even when the effects of socioeconomic development are accounted for. Cross-sectional regressions indicate that effective programs have a smaller effect than such factors as rising levels of female education but still reduce fertility—net of such other factors—by perhaps one-and-a-half births per woman. Skeptics put the reduction at only one birth instead but do not deny it exists (Pritchett, 1994a, 1994b). The reduction is in the region of 40 percent of the fertility decline in developing countries from the 1960s to the end of the 1980s (Bongaarts, forthcoming).

Cross-national statistical analysis, like experimental work, therefore indicates that family planning programs contribute to contraceptive use and lower fertility. But both types of studies agree that the contribution is contingent. Programs are not uniformly successful; their effects are influenced by the social context (level of development, cultural factors, political support) and depend on program performance (on the quality of program effort, the design of interventions, the adequacy of supervision of service providers, etc.). A brief overview of these factors affecting program effectiveness helps clarify when and why programs work.

SOCIOECONOMIC AND CULTURAL FACTORS

Socioeconomic factors are not always favorable when national programs are launched. Does it follow that programs have to wait for incomes to grow, education levels to rise, and cities to come to dominate the countryside before they have any effect? Apparently not. No socioeconomic thresholds are evident in such data as those in Table 2. Fertility decline started in East Asia, in the 1960s and

Table 2

Socioeconomic Indicators at the Start of Fertility Transition, Selected Countries, and Comparative Aggregate Data

Region and Country	Start of Fertility Transition[a]	GNP per Capita[b]	Infant Mortality Rate	Female Secondary Enrollment	Percent Urban	Start of Population Program
East Asia						
Indonesia	1975	253	109	15	19	1968
Korea, Rep. of	1960	550	70	14	28	1961
Philippines	1970	488	66	50	33	1970
Thailand	1970	471	73	15	13	1970
South Asia						
Bangladesh	1975	138	138	11	9	1971
India	1965	218	150	13	19	1965
Pakistan	1985	304	113	8	30	1960
Sri Lanka	1965	216	63	35	20	1965
Latin America						
Brazil	1965	889	104	16	50	1974
Colombia	1965	676	86	16	54	1970
Costa Rica	1965	1,109	72	25	38	1968
Mexico	1975	1,504	64	28	63	1974
Sub-Saharan Africa						
Botswana	1980	721	63	22	15	1971
Kenya	1980	358	83	16	16	1967
Zimbabwe	1970	544	96	6	17	1968

Table 2—Continued

Region and Country	Start of Fertility Transition[a]	GNP per Capita[b]	Infant Mortality Rate	Female Secondary Enrollment	Percent Urban	Start of Population Program
Comparative data (1995)[c]						
Low-income economies (except China and India)		290	89	21	28	
Lower-middle income economies		1,670	41	62	56	
Upper-middle income economies		4,260	35	75	73	

SOURCES: World Bank (1993, pp. 20–21). Comparative data from World Bank (1996, 1997b).

[a]Fertility transitions are dated from initial declines of at least 0.7 points in total fertility over a five-year period, following Bulatao and Elwan (1985).

[b]Constant 1987 U.S. dollars. These and the other indicators are as of the transition date, except for the comparative data, which are given as of 1995.

[c]Female enrollment is as of 1993. The enrollment figure for upper-middle-income economies is the median across 13 countries.

1970s, at income levels typical of low-income economies today. In Indonesia, in particular, GNP per capita was about US$250, which is below the mean level for low-income economies. Even lower income levels were typical of South Asian countries at the start of their transitions. Latin America was different, with a number of countries not starting transitions until reaching much higher income levels, up to US$1,500 per capita. Where transitions have started most recently, in sub-Saharan Africa, income levels at the start were intermediate between Asian and Latin American levels.

The changes in personal aspirations and in the acceptability of family planning that trigger fertility transition appear to have occurred at many different socioeconomic levels. For the countries in Table 2, fertility transition started at infant mortality levels as high as 150 deaths per thousand or as low as 63[2]; where female secondary enrollment was only 6 percent or already 50 percent; and where anywhere from 9 percent to 63 percent of the population was urban. Fertility transition can therefore start with social indicators practically anywhere in the range typical of low-income or even lower-middle-income economies, with no specific levels triggering decline.

Nevertheless, socioeconomic development does contribute to lower fertility. Cross-national comparisons suggest that the pace of decline, once it has started, is faster in more advanced developing countries (Bongaarts and Watkins, 1996), either because higher levels of development condition people to be more favorable to smaller families or because they allow programs to operate more efficiently. And once the transition is under way, contraceptive use appears to spread in a diffusion process that takes on a life of its own.

If low levels of socioeconomic development do not deter family planning programs, neither do cultural obstacles. Skeptics have cited one obstacle or another practically everywhere programs were launched. None appears to be an effective impediment. In East Asia the cultural barriers included Confucian traditions (in Taiwan and South Korea) that made the family central and gave household heads control over extended families, including the childbearing of their children. A strong preference for sons to carry on the family line has

---

[2]But see Bulatao and Elwan (1985) for a possible mortality threshold (see also Bongaarts and Watkins, 1996).

also often been cited. Political opposition of various sorts has existed to family planning, for instance among Islamic fundamentalists in Indonesia and the Catholic hierarchy in the Philippines. Such opposition was even more important in Latin America. Although the predominant Catholicism did not deter couples from voluntarily adopting contraception, the opposition of the church legitimized intellectual opposition to limiting population growth. In addition, the split in many Latin American countries between the dominant elite and the peasant masses slowed the spread of contraception. In South Asia, the barriers included such factors as traditional family structures, the subordinate social position of women, and continuing dependence on child labor. Similar barriers have been adduced for sub-Saharan Africa, where decisions on childbearing have been assumed to be controlled by older generations who consider children and grandchildren essential assets.

Yet in each of these settings, despite the cultural obstacles and despite varying and often low socioeconomic levels, some degree of interest in smaller families or demand for contraception appears to have existed. Near the start of fertility transition in South Korea, Thailand, and Indonesia, ideal family size was recorded at around four children, already below existing fertility. For a number of Latin American countries, substantial demand for contraception probably exceeded the capacity of early programs. Even in Bangladesh, substantial "latent demand" appears to have existed, with fertility preferences similar to those in other Asian countries at a similar stage of fertility transition (Cleland et al., 1994, p. 48). Sub-Saharan Africa initially presents a different picture, with large families still often highly prized, but in this region considerable interest exists in spacing births.

PROGRAM STRATEGIES AND APPROACHES

Though neither socioeconomic development nor cultural and institutional factors determine program success, sensitivity to such factors does seem to be a hallmark of successful programs. Where they have succeeded—and at least some successes have been recorded in every region of the developing world—programs have built on existing demand for contraception and have experimented to develop ways to address socioeconomic and cultural obstacles.

In East Asia, existing demand was exploited in pilot projects that demonstrated widespread desire for contraception, such as the large-scale Taichung project in Taiwan and the Jakarta pilot project in Indonesia. Close attention to the demand was evident in recurrent surveys in Taiwan to learn about attitudes toward family planning. Political support was a benefit of such demonstrations, although support also developed for different reasons, not always within the control of programs. Delivery systems for family planning eventually became massive and well organized in each country but not before extensive experimentation with various means of delivery. Thailand tested optimal delivery systems in the Potharam project; Korea experimented with urban programs in Sundong Gu and rural programs in Koyang. Eventually, "Mothers' Clubs" became an important element of the Korean program, used in rural areas to mobilize support for smaller families and to motivate women to adopt family planning while assisting with such concerns as income generation (Cho et al., 1982, pp. 129–131). An existing institutional capacity to mobilize peasants was also critical in Indonesia, where an aggressive program drew on a local government structure strengthened after the 1965 coup attempt (McNicoll, 1983, p. 86) and worked intensively with community groups.

Facing even stronger demand in Latin America coupled with barriers to government involvement, programs evolved in a different way. Demand for contraception was initially met by physicians; by commercial sales; and, increasingly, by private voluntary organizations, such as *Profamilia* in Colombia. Discovering substantial latent demand (Tamayo, 1989), *Profamilia* began with urban clinics and expanded after a few years into community-based rural services and also began offering sterilization. The government tolerated the provision of services, probably recognizing the widespread demand for them. Demonstration of this demand was critical in the eventual institution of government services, which eclipsed private services in Mexico. In Colombia, private services continue to be more important; in Brazil, the private organization *Sociedade Bem-Estar Familiar no Brasil* (BEMFAM) remains a major provider, partly as a contractor to state governments. Experimentation with delivery options has often involved the private sector. With large nationally coordinated programs coming late to the region, contraceptive growth has been slower in Latin America than in East Asia.

South Asia illustrates both initial obliviousness to demand and eventual responsiveness to it. The early spread of contraception was retarded by programs that were heavily bureaucratic and largely administered from the top, especially in Pakistan, where little attempt was made to gauge client demand, and little attention was paid to the needs of front-line staff. The Indian program is harder to characterize because of its diversity and some degree of control by individual states. In general, however, the Indian program also failed to capitalize on all the existing and potential demand for contraception and focused narrowly on sterilization. Targets were set high in the hierarchy, and officials at the top were largely out of touch with village life (Freedman, 1990, p. 39).

In contrast, the program in Sri Lanka, the only one in the region that showed some early success, was much more sensitive to client needs. The Sri Lanka program provided a wide range of methods, including such temporary methods as pills and IUDs, and used community-based distributors in rural areas. The Indian program, on the other hand, focused initially on the IUD and later largely on sterilization, avoiding community distribution of other methods, and experimented instead (to a much greater extent than in Sri Lanka) with incentives and controls on age at marriage, measures with theoretical appeal but limited practical attraction to individuals. The Indian program had more striking political support and better advertising, but the Sri Lankan program delivered the contraceptives. Much more similar to the Sri Lankan approach was the program in Bangladesh as it evolved after 1975. Assuming the existence of latent demand, it focused on mitigating the costs to individuals, both practical and psychic, of using contraception. Frequent contact by trained and caring workers with clients was emphasized, often in the clients' own homes to overcome cultural restrictions on women's mobility. As with earlier programs in East Asia, substantial experimentation with delivery alternatives has gone on in the Matlab area and through the succeeding Extension project (Cleland et al., 1994), with coordinated funding from many international donors.

In the sub-Saharan countries that have made the most progress in reducing fertility—Botswana, Zimbabwe, and Kenya—programs address existing demand for child spacing by providing temporary methods, mainly the pill. Delivery systems have been quite different, however. Botswana, with presumably stronger demand in a relatively more developed setting with a public health system that covers the country fairly extensively, has relied largely on health posts and health centers to provide contraceptives. Zimbabwe placed primary emphasis on community-based distribution to reach out to the rural population. Kenya has also emphasized outreach but has relied to a much greater extent than Zimbabwe on private voluntary organizations to complement public services.

The key to a successful program therefore appears to lie less in a favorable environment than in what the program does with the material it has. No socioeconomic setting, however impoverished, appears devoid of some demand for controlling fertility; even in the most favorable environments, some groups will have unmet need for contraception. Government programs, properly run and complemented where appropriate with private efforts, do appear capable of identifying and satisfying demand, although encouragement and substantial support from international donors has been virtually continual in these cases. Demand for controlling fertility can be fragile and variable; given that family planning is often a sensitive topic, initial approaches need to be tailored to each setting.

THE BASICS OF PROGRAM SUCCESS

Beyond the general willingness and ability to unearth and respond to existing demand—whatever the form—are there specific structures, activities, or approaches essential for program success? In 1964, Bernard Berelson, a major figure in the population movement, proposed a set of requirements that have been expanded over time into the 30 items that give the family planning program effort score previously mentioned. The 30 items—shown grouped into sets in Table 3 in accordance with factor analysis results—are widely recognized as indicators of serious organizational effort.

The first two sets of items are central and essential. First, adequate program effort means providing access to a variety of contraceptive methods—pills, condoms, IUDs, sterilization—to meet the varying needs and preferences of couples. To provide such access, a good logistical system is needed. In addition—as the second set of items indicates—effective contraceptive provision requires managing the front-line providers: They have to be trained, made to focus on their

Table 3

Family Planning Program Effort Items

Item	Description
Method access	
Pills access	Proportion with easy access to pills or injectables
Condom access	Proportion with easy access to condoms, diaphragms, or spermicides
IUD access	Proportion with easy access to IUDs
Female sterilization	Availability of female sterilization and proportion with easy access
Male sterilization	Availability of male sterilization and proportion with easy access
Logistics	How frequently stocks of supplies and equipment are adequate
Management	
Training programs	Adequacy of staff training programs
Tasks execution	How well all staff categories carry out assigned tasks
Recordkeeping	Whether client records are kept, summarized, and fed back to clinics
Managers use evaluation	Extent of use by program managers of evaluation and research results to improve program
Evaluation	Whether program-related demographic and operations research are conducted and whether staff or other institutions exist for this purpose
Supervision	Adequacy of supervision at all levels
Mobilization	
Government policy	Whether government officially supports family planning and population control
Public statements	Whether high officials publicly state support for family planning
Rank of leader	Rank in the bureaucracy of the family planning leadership
Other ministries	Involvement in population activities of ministries and government agencies without primary responsibility for service delivery
Civil bureaucracy used	Use of civil bureaucracy (including central, provincial, district, and county administrators) to ensure program directives are carried out
Incentives	Whether incentives and disincentives are provided to clients or staff
Marketing	
Advertising restrictions	Freedom from restriction of contraceptive advertising in mass media
Social marketing	Extent of coverage by subsidized commercial contraceptive sales
Media coverage	Frequency and coverage of mass media messages

Table 3—Continued

Item	Description
Medical approaches	
Abortion access	Proportion with easy access to abortion under good conditions
Postpartum programs	Extent of coverage by postpartum programs
In-country budget	Proportion of family planning budget provided from country sources
Missionary approaches	
Community distribution	Extent of coverage by community-based contraceptive distribution programs
Private agencies	Involvement of private-sector agencies and groups
Home visitors	Extent of coverage by family planning workers who visit women's homes
Other	
Administrative structure	Adequacy of national, provincial, and county administrative structure and staff
Age-at-marriage policy	How high the minimum legal marriage age for women is and how strongly it is enforced
Import laws	Whether laws facilitate contraceptive imports or local manufacture

SOURCES: Descriptions abridged from Mauldin and Lapham (1985, pp. 8-10). See Bulatao (1996) for grouping of items.

assigned tasks, motivated to keep essential records on their clients, and properly supervised in their duties. A good management system that accomplishes these things will also periodically assess progress and use evaluation results to improve operations.

The third set of items has to do with mobilization of government resources to support family planning. Six items reflect this: the adoption of a national population policy; supportive public statements from political leaders; the rank accorded to the program leadership within the government bureaucracy; the involvement of other ministries besides the service delivery agency itself[3]; the involvement of the civil bureaucracy at regional, provincial, and local levels; and the provision of incentives or disincentives to family planning clients

---

[3]These could include the health ministry, if it is not the primary service provider; the prime minister's office or its equivalent; and a host of other ministries in the areas of social security, planning and development, finance, interior, education, environment, youth and sports, transport, defense, women's affairs, mass media and information, foreign affairs, rural development, urban affairs, religious affairs, and social affairs.

or staff. This set of items is somewhat problematic; official support is essential in obtaining program resources but can easily shade into official pressure. In fact, the last item, the provision of incentives, needs to be carefully handled so as not to lead to undue influence on potential clients (Isaacs, 1995).

More consistently important than mobilization is program activity to reach the population with appropriate messages (the fourth set of items), especially through mass media, advertising, and commercial sales. The last two sets of items reflect delivery-system alternatives chosen in some but not other cases: clinic-based or largely "medical" alternatives, such as postpartum programs and abortion, and outreach systems, often with a strong volunteer component, such as community-based distribution, private agencies, and home visitation.

Rather than strict program requirements, a number of these items are alternatives that may be more or less important in particular settings. Few programs receive high scores across all these areas, and even some quite successful programs do little in some areas. In Bangladesh, for instance, where an extensive review of experience concludes that program-promoted changes in acceptability and availability of contraception have been much more responsible for fertility decline than any changes in preferred family size, a few of the items just discussed were identified as critical (Cleland et al., 1994, pp. 97, 122):

- an organizational culture of excellence, stressing dedication to realistic goals and "insulating the workforce from dysfunctional social pressures"

- frequent contact with clients by outreach workers with basic technical skills and strong supervision

- reliable supply of multiple methods and available follow-up and ancillary services.

The essential elements of organizational effort may vary not only by setting but also by stage of development of the program. Table 4 indicates the stages a program goes through, drawing on several

Table 4

Stages in Program Development

Initial Level of Family Planning Effort	Dominant Concern	Client Focus	Main Source of Support	Extensiveness of Program Functioning
Very weak (0–24)	Promotion	Highly moti-vated couples	Donors and voluntary organiza-tions	Very few sites
Weak (25–54)	Management	Couples with unmet demand	Government	Limited cov-erage
Moderate (55–79)	Outreach	Broad popula-tions	Government	Extensive coverage
Strong (80+)	Efficiency	Least accessi-ble popula-tions	Clients	Increasingly selective cov-erage

SOURCE: World Bank (1993).

schemes suggested by researchers (Bulatao, 1993; Vriesendorp et al., 1989; Keller et al., 1989; Townsend, 1991; Bernhart, 1991).

The evidence that program actions in each of these areas contribute to success is varied and complex (and not without occasional contradictions). Some evidence will be briefly reviewed, covering the provision of access to methods and satisfaction of other client needs, management issues, promotion through the media, delivery systems, and political and financial support.

Responding to Client Needs

Consider first some of the evidence that a program that responds to client needs increases contraceptive use:

- *Improved access to services helps clients.* Access can vary greatly: Some countries may have only one service point for 15,000 women; in others, every community may have at least one such facility. Such variation in proximity to services, according to a review of 16 studies that differ widely in methodology, does affect contraceptive use, even controlling for other factors (Tsui and

Ochoa, 1989; Angeles et al., 1996). Expanding access when contraceptive use is still limited is especially important (Phillips et al., 1994).

- *Facilities or field-workers must, of course, have contraceptive supplies available.* This is often an obstacle in newer programs, such as several in sub-Saharan Africa that suffer from supply shortages and inadequate logistical planning (UNFPA, 1990). Providing not only reliable supplies but also a wider range of appropriate methods increases use. In the Philippines, for instance, providing an additional method through clinics raises prevalence by 5 percentage points (Samara et al., 1996, p. 48). Increasing method choice need not be costly; data from Bangladesh suggest that adding reversible methods to a program that relies heavily on sterilization need not raise the cost per birth prevented (Simmons et al., 1991).

- *Measures that promote continued use are also helpful.* Improved counseling and better client information, for instance, lead to better method choices, fewer complaints about side effects, less-frequent discontinuation (WHO, 1980), fewer method failures, and less need for abortion. But the possible choices still have drawbacks that discourage some women, although others persevere despite them. Focus-group researchers quote one woman in Karachi as saying: "There is pain in these methods, but at least there is no danger that the woman will conceive" (Snow et al., n.d.). Research to improve contraceptive methods and develop new ones is still critical and requires continued public-sector funding (Harrison and Rosenfield, 1996).

- *Whether ancillary services should also be provided is a complicated issue involving difficult trade-offs.* Clients have other needs and demands besides contraception, and a program that can address these may be more effective and may also make critical contributions in such related areas as the attempt to contain the human immunodeficiency virus (HIV) and the acquired immunodeficiency syndrome (AIDS).[4] Some added services, including

---

[4]Attempts at integrating services for sexually transmitted infections (STIs) with family planning, as in Mombasa, Kenya (Twahir et al., 1996), and eastern Uganda (Mukaire et al., 1997), suggest that there are advantages for family planning programs in offering more services, but also difficulties posed by the increased responsibilities. Serious

pregnancy tests, Pap smears, and screening for sexually transmitted diseases, are sufficiently integral to providing contraception that their role in a clinical program is clear. Other services
range farther afield, from emergency obstetric services to
income-generating activities for women and female education.
Certainly desirable themselves, such activities may also promote
lower fertility preferences, and combining them with family
planning may have synergistic effects. Recognizing such arguments, the 1994 International Conference on Population and
Development in Cairo supported the idea of family planning as
one among various reproductive health interventions, all to be
pursued together. However, ancillary interventions increase
program costs, in some cases (as with emergency obstetric services) by quite substantial amounts, and additional financing is
seldom easily available. Family planning program staff are not
necessarily the proper people to provide ancillary services. Integrating such staff into larger health organizations risks submerg-
ing concerns about family planning, which seldom receive adequate attention within health ministries (Finkle and Ness, 1985).
For these reasons, the debate about "vertical" (stand-alone) family planning programs versus integrated programs run as part of
health ministries has continued unresolved for decades. A series
of careful quasi-experiments in Bangladesh concludes that

> minimal health provision indeed may indirectly benefit contracep-
> tive acceptance. However, the addition of a broader range of health
> skills and supplies made no further impact on the success of family
> planning. Rather there was evidence of a drop in contraceptive use
> as the attention and energies of workers were diverted. . . . Integra-
> tion must be justified on grounds other than enhanced family
> planning effectiveness (Cleland et al., 1994, p. 146).

The issue of what services to combine with family planning therefore
remains to be approached in each case as a matter of values and
objectives, but with full awareness of the practical consequences.[5]

---

questions also remain about the accuracy of STI diagnoses and the cost-effectiveness
of integrated services (Maggwa and Askew, 1997).

[5]See Tsui, Wasserheit, and Haaga (1997, pp. 158–163) for a further discussion of the
issues from the perspective of reproductive health services—a discussion that does
not, however, appear to come to a clear conclusion.

Managing Effectively

Elements of good management also contribute to more contraceptive use. Informal comparisons of national programs easily demonstrate this, but it is difficult to control complicating factors. More precise evidence therefore usually comes from experiments or small studies.

* *Training can improve provider performance.* This is an article of faith for most programs. Several hundred short-term training courses in family planning and maternal health are conducted each year around the world in more than two dozen different languages. Studies in such countries as Bangladesh, Ecuador, Morocco, and Ghana confirm that trained field-workers and supervisors perform better (Finkle and Ness, 1985; Gallen and Rinehart, 1986, p. 825; Brown et al., 1995), and other studies indicate the need for periodic retraining (Gallen and Rinehart, 1986, p. 826). Training does have to match the specific provider's needs, reflect actual problems and options, emphasize practical skills, and focus on developing competence.

* *Good supervision is often cited as a central element in program success*, given the many shortcomings of supervisors who must labor under "low salaries, harsh working conditions, and the absence of performance-based rewards" and are distracted by administrative requirements and their own pressing personal affairs (Simmons, 1987, p. 251). Studies in Nigeria, Guatemala, Turkey, and Brazil (Townsend, 1991, p. 55; Foreit and Foreit, 1984) indicate that frequent supervisory visits increase program effectiveness. What supervisory visits cover is critical: Providing training and reinforcement and actually observing worker contacts have much more effect than merely collecting management information.

* *Strategic planning, aided by reliable evaluation data and good applied research into program options* (usually referred to as "operations research"), *contributes to program success.* The East Asian experience, in which extensive field experiments and continuing research and evaluation were used to guide program expansion (as well as to generate public support), and the similar experience in Bangladesh suggest the importance of these factors. Reviews of development programs similarly suggest the

importance of strategic planning or strategic management (Paul, 1983), which requires sensitivity to the environment a program faces.

Targeting services to those most in need, or collecting some payment from those who can afford it, is a sensible option that can improve financial sustainability. Nominal price increases do not appear to affect contraceptive use substantially, as studies of price elasticities in Jamaica and in several Southeast Asian countries suggest (Lewis, 1996). However, the time and the manner for introducing such changes require careful consideration in each case, especially so they do not affect the poor (Lande and Geller, 1991).

Promoting Family Planning

Promotional activities to reach the public, particularly through mass media, can have substantial effect but have to be properly done. Brief 30-second "spots" in Peru had only a small effect (Westoff et al., 1994). In contrast, continuing publicity about family planning had a greater effect in India. A large national survey established that exposure to a family planning message in the past month increased the number intending to use contraceptives by 6 percentage points, controlling for socioeconomic factors and for general media exposure (Ramesh et al., 1996). Finally, an extensive media campaign in Nigeria, with radio and TV dramas, music videos with popular artists, billboards, bumper stickers, and so on, demonstrated a clear effect on behavior. Among those exposed to media messages in 1990, almost twice as many were using contraception three years later than among those not exposed. The influence of exposure appeared more often among those who then discussed family planning issues with current users and was greater on initial adoption than on continuation. Media exposure also appeared responsible for reducing fertility preferences by about half a child (Bankole et al., 1996; Bankole and Adewuyi, 1994). Advertising in particular can make a difference: Condom sales are more closely linked to advertising than to any other factor (Boone et al., 1985).

Selecting a Delivery System

The major distinctions among delivery systems are between clinic-based delivery, community-based distribution (or outreach systems more generally), and commercial distribution. An overlapping distinction may also be made between public and private distribution, although private systems may involve some degree of public subsidy. These different systems are often complementary:

- Clinics are needed for such methods as sterilization and to provide backup for outreach workers and referral, when needed, for clients' medical problems. Proximity to clinics increases contraceptive use, as noted earlier, up to the point at which clinics and other facilities are easily accessible to everyone.

- Community-based distribution involves bringing contraceptives to women in their own communities, rather than requiring them to travel to clinics. Such efforts are especially needed where clinics are too sparse and too expensive to build and maintain. They often depend on local residents with a few weeks' training, who receive no fixed salary but may have various incentives. Their effectiveness at increasing contraceptive use has been demonstrated in many countries, including Egypt, Mexico, the Democratic Republic of Congo, and Bangladesh (Gallen and Rinehart, 1986; Bertrand, 1991). However, at higher levels of contraceptive prevalence in Brazil and the Eastern Caribbean, community-based distribution had minimal effect. With the large workforce they require, the costs of community-based distribution can be a concern. These costs can vary from US$5 to US$150 per user per year (Huber and Harvey, 1989). For each setting in which outreach is needed, the most cost-effective way to provide outreach needs to be considered.

- Distributing partly subsidized contraceptives through commercial channels, aided by catchy advertising, has become known as contraceptive social marketing. This provides an alternative source of supply, especially for condoms and pills, that can be more congenial for some users and therefore can expand contraceptive use. To the extent these are new users or switch from government programs, the considerably lower cost of social marketing saves public funds; however, users may also switch from purely commercial outlets.

- Private voluntary organizations operate a range of distribution systems, some involving clinics and others concentrating on outreach. Volunteer programs have been critical in introducing family planning in various settings and are still useful for reaching specific target groups, such as adolescents, and for providing some competition and some savings to government programs.

- Additional delivery systems of many types often coexist with these. Private physicians and midwives often provide some contraceptive services on their own, although they would often benefit from specific training in family planning. Health insurance or other employer-supported programs may cover contraceptive services. Commercial outlets may be better or worse at supplying contraceptives. Since expanding service outlets and generally making family planning more available lead to increased contraceptive use, the multiplication of such distribution systems can be useful, and public programs should be designed to complement rather than to discourage them.[6]

Mobilizing Support

Political support is essential to enable a program in such a sensitive area as family planning to achieve respectability and have sustained effect. Programs depend on politically allocated resources. At least as important, they also depend on a positive, widespread popular response, which is greatly aided by visible political support. Government endorsement of family planning helps legitimize what is initially innovative behavior and can helpfully be supplemented by support from the media, voluntary organizations, and even religious groups. Official support has grown over the decades and is now close to universal, but the depth of this support and the extent to which it is reflected in effective government action still vary considerably.

Government support does have to be tempered to preserve voluntary individual choice. This is important not only to protect human rights but also for pragmatic reasons. Coercive programs cannot succeed or even survive for long in countries that aspire to be democratic. India attempted to force sterilizations after emergency rule was declared in the mid-1970s; partly as a result, the government was soon voted out of office. The most coercive modern program was

---

[6]See World Bank (1993a, pp. 68–69) for an example of how commercial services can be disrupted by a public program.

launched in China by a government intent on controlling every aspect of life, including childbearing. China is the only country that has "penalized people specifically and directly for violating population policy" (Li, 1995, p. 563). Yet the Chinese one-child policy has been remarkably ineffective. An analysis of fertility in Hebei and Tianjin (around the capital) concludes that "The majority of Chinese women . . . ignored birth-quota regulations, refused to accept the one-child certificate, and bore the burden of heavy financial penalties" (Li, 1995, p. 582). International donors have generally turned away from such coercive programs and have been increasingly active in improving the quality and service orientation of the programs they assist.

International donors have played an important role in helping to marshal government support for voluntary family planning programs. They have done this not only through financial assistance for services but also through political dialogue, at successive world population conferences for instance (Bucharest in 1974, Mexico City in 1984, Cairo in 1994), which allowed a consensus to build in favor of family planning. Donors have also largely underwritten such activities as the World Fertility Survey and the Demographic and Health Surveys and contributed to various rounds of national censuses, which have demonstrated to governments the specific population-growth scenarios they face. Donor influence in initiating and strengthening programs has been substantial, as has been argued by such observers as Warwick (1982, p. 44), who states that, at least through the 1980s, "of all the spheres of national development, population has been the most donor driven."

Some impact of donor funding on ongoing programs appears in statistical analysis, although not consistently. In comparisons across Asian countries up to the early 1980s, Ness and Ando (1984) found that the volume of outside financial aid did not affect program strength. But more recently, Tsui (1997) has shown that, across all recipient countries, population assistance from the United States (through USAID, the agency responsible for bilateral foreign-aid programs) has a small but significant impact on program effort. The inconclusive statistical evidence is understandable: donors naturally are selective in their assistance, sometimes choosing more promising settings, sometimes more impoverished ones, and often ones with which they have some special cultural or political link. This makes interpretation difficult.

Anecdotal evidence and experience suggest several ways in which donor influence has been important to ongoing programs:

- in providing the training and developing the technical and managerial resources on which programs rely

- in encouraging new approaches, from new contraceptive methods, such as implants, to new strategies, such as community-based distribution and social marketing

- in sponsoring research into ways to make programs work better, research that nascent programs seldom can spend their own time and resources on

- in encouraging service standards in such areas as the need for informed consent.

Donor involvement in a program is not a guarantee of success, but it provides resources that, coupled with national commitment and a reasonable strategy, can accelerate the progress of a program.

Chapter Four

THE COST OF FAMILY PLANNING

Expenditures on family planning across all developing countries are under US$10 billion, much of it paid by national governments or individual households. Equivalent to around US$1–2 per person per year, this is not large by many standards. Family planning is a cheap way to reduce fertility, although other approaches are also worth pursuing simultaneously. Governments have several good reasons to support family planning programs, for the benefits they provide users and the society as a whole. Donor countries also have a stake in moderating global population growth, with its threats to the environment, to economic progress, and to political stability in many critical regions. Although they do not cover the bulk of the costs, donor contributions have been critical in the past and continue to be indispensable.

PUBLIC EXPENDITURES

Public expenditures on family planning in developing countries were estimated by several sources for 1990 at US$4–5 billion and are somewhat higher now (World Bank, 1993a). However, these estimates are difficult to make with confidence. Apart from the vagaries of government budgetary data in developing countries, the estimates are complicated by the difficulty of separating family planning from other health services, by the multiplicity of agencies involved in family planning and the many channels through which they may be funded, and to some extent by the definition of what activities should be counted. For the Cairo population conference, UNFPA (1994) estimated the cost of family planning programs in the year 2000 at US$10.2 billion and then added US$5.0 billion for reproductive services that can be provided as part of primary health care; US$1.3 billion for prevention of sexually transmitted diseases, including HIV/AIDS; and US$600 million for population data collection, analysis, and policy development.[1]

Expenditures are usually tied to the number of users and are expected to grow as the reproductive-age population grows—by about 2 percent a year currently, although the rate will slow to 1 percent around 2015. But one also has to allow for changing program costs. The initial years of a program require the heaviest investment; as the number of contraceptive users grows, it can become easier to serve them. But additional expenditures may be necessary to maintain the program's momentum and to reach new user groups, as well as to improve service quality and expand related reproductive health services.

Public family planning expenditures are quite variable across countries in comparison to public expenditures on health. Estimates around 1989 suggest that family planning is most often around 2 percent of the government health budget. However, many of the countries covered in these estimates have quite weak programs, and the proportion goes up to 20–30 percent for some extensive (and successful) programs, such as those in Indonesia and Bangladesh (Ross et al., 1993). Some countries have therefore had considerable scope to fund their family planning programs out of health budgets, but others have required considerable outside assistance.

Funds from international donors cover a fourth to a third of public expenditures on family planning throughout the developing world (the overall proportion is low because China and India provide so much of their own family planning resources). Donor commitments—designated support for population and family planning from

---

[1]Agency estimates of needed resources in their areas should normally be treated with caution and some skepticism. The family planning cost estimate appears somewhat high in comparison with 1990 estimates (on which there is reasonable consensus), but the reproductive health-services cost estimate is undoubtedly far too low. Various joint costs are counted under family planning rather than reproductive health (and further development of the methodology for apportioning costs is needed). In addition, the estimates for reproductive health are not meant to cover emergency obstetric services above the primary health-care level, which are critical in reducing maternal mortality. No comparable estimates of overall costs developed independently of funding agencies are available.

industrial countries, as well as funds passing through multilateral institutions and development banks, plus funds from private donors—fluctuate from year to year. They appeared to increase substantially, to US$1.37 billion, the year after the 1994 Cairo conference (as they did after the previous world conference in 1984). However, comparisons are complicated by the expanded mandate from the Cairo conference to tackle reproductive health, funding for which was counted for the first time in 1995 and found to comprise 23 percent of donor commitments. Not counting such funding, donor commitments actually fell from 1994 to 1995 (by 7 percent in real terms; funding trends in current dollars are shown in Figure 13). Even counting reproductive health funding, substantially larger increases will be needed to meet the Cairo conference goal of donor support for a third of the cost of population and reproductive health programs by 2000 (UNFPA, 1997b).

Per capita, developing countries receive US$0.15 from international donors for population and reproductive health programs, but regional variation is considerable. Sub-Saharan Africa (with its rela-

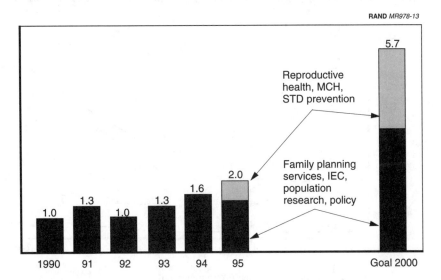

RAND MR978-13

SOURCE: UNFPA (forthcoming) for trend and UNFPA (1994) for goal.

Figure 13—Trend in Donor Assistance for Population
Programs and Goal for 2000 (billion U.S. $)

tively newer programs and smaller populations) receives more and absorbed almost 80 percent of the increases in 1995, and Asia (with older programs and larger populations) receives less (Figure 14).

Government and donors do not cover all the costs of family planning. Households pick up some proportion of the costs, about as much as donors do, by one earlier estimate (Bulatao, 1985). In countries where commercial contraceptive supply is limited, the contraceptives available are unaffordable for most. But prices at pharmacies and smaller outlets decline as the number of users increases, and price decreases do stimulate demand (Lewis, 1985). The cost of public programs also goes down. The cost per user of program-supplied modern methods may be estimated roughly at US$20, but may range from US$50 to under US$15 as the number of contraceptive users increases (Figure 15).

To assess whether there are cheaper ways to reduce fertility, comparisons are sometimes made between family planning and other development interventions. For instance, the cost-effectiveness of family planning for reducing fertility has been contrasted with that of

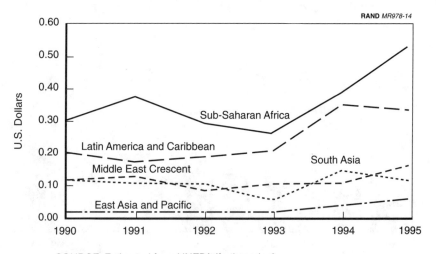

SOURCE: Estimated from UNFPA (forthcoming).

Figure 14—Trend in What Developing Regions Receive per Capita in Donor Support for Population Programs (constant 1990 U.S. $)

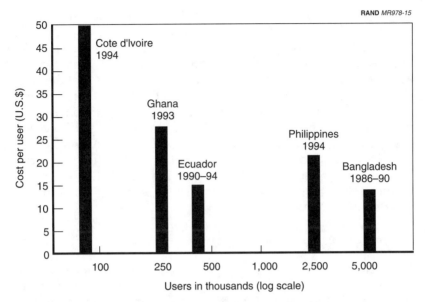

SOURCE: Unpublished studies of the EVALUATION Project at the University of North Carolina at Chapel Hill.

Figure 15—Program Cost per Contraceptive User by Number of Users, Selected Countries

primary schooling for girls in 16 countries, mostly Asian and Latin American. The median cost of averting a birth through a family planning program, at US$58, was much lower than the median cost of averting a birth through female education, at US$548 (Cochrane, 1988).[2] A similar comparison of family planning with several child-survival initiatives, including immunization, maternal and child health programs, and infant and child feeding programs, gave a similar result. The lowest-cost alternative among these mortality-reduction initiatives was still more expensive, per birth averted, than family planning, with only one exception across countries (measles immunization in Kenya). The median cost for family planning was again about a tenth of the median cost for mortality reduction (Cochrane and Zachariah, 1983).

---

[2]Average costs were used because marginal costs were not available.

Such comparisons are seriously limited, since only the fertility effect, not the other effects of the interventions, is taken into account.[3] What they point to, nevertheless, is the inability of general education and health programs to satisfy unmet need directly. Instead, they create over time a general desire for smaller families and the social climate in which such desires can be realized and therefore are a useful complement to family planning programs and have contributed powerfully to fertility decline. But their effects involve long lags: The long delay between a girl's schooling and her childbearing, and the many things that must intervene to allow her to limit her fertility, as opposed to the relatively immediate effects of family planning programs, account for the latter's advantage in such comparisons as those above.

GOVERNMENT INVOLVEMENT

There are several arguments for government support of family planning—the utility of family planning programs for reducing fertility, the opportunities that lower fertility and dependency rates, and the resulting increased saving rates and reduced growth of expenditures on social programs. Paradoxically, however, these arguments are less compelling for poorer countries, which would benefit less because the amounts they could save are smaller relative to the cost of programs. In addition, any gains from family planning are strictly contingent, dependent first on the programs being well-run, and then on any opportunities opened up by lower fertility—for expanding enrollment, for instance—being used productively. This requires effective governance, which tends to be more difficult in more constrained environments.

In a different sense, however, government involvement in family planning is more critical in poorer countries. Commercial services

---

[3]Knowles (1997) considers this "the main shortcoming of this type of analysis . . . that the alternative investments compared to family planning provide a wide range of private and social benefits not incorporated into the analysis, so that the exercise risks being irrelevant." Arguably, however, family planning also provides a range of other benefits besides lower fertility, such as reduced mortality (for which its cost-effectiveness is noted below). Knowles does make other important points in his broad critique of such work, noting, for instance, that the alternatives to government financing are seldom clearly modeled. In addition, data for comparative analyses, such as the specific ones cited, always have some deficiencies.

are less likely to be available and more likely to be beyond the reach of individuals. Furthermore, family planning improves maternal and child health. By reducing exposure to pregnancy, family planning reduces maternal deaths at a cost below that of such programs as prenatal care and training of traditional birth attendants, particularly for poorer countries where maternal mortality rates are high (Maine, 1991). The cost per child death averted by a model family planning program is also quite low, being estimated at US$4–5 per added year of life in Mali, a poorer country, and at US$25 per added year in Mexico or Thailand. This is as cheap or cheaper than a model immunization program, which costs three times as much (US$12–17) per added year of life in lower-income countries and slightly more (US$25–30) in middle-income countries.[4] Family planning services are therefore recommended as part of a primary health care package ensured for the entire population, most strongly although not only for poorer countries (World Bank, 1993b).

Whether to save money, to save lives, to guarantee reproductive rights and the reproductive health of women, or to temper environmental and social problems, governments in both the poorer and the more advanced developing countries, wherever fertility remains high, have strong reasons for financial support of family planning. Such support need not mean government provision of services. Many successful programs have been government run, but many government-run programs have also languished for years. Where appropriate private agencies exist or can be nurtured into existence, they could in principle take on some of this burden, with some public support, and enhance the performance of programs. But government does have an essential role in ensuring appropriate public education and an adequate flow of information about family planning, as well as in guaranteeing proper standards of care. Addressing both of these tasks adequately—which the private sector is generally not equipped to do—could help mitigate unfamiliarity with contra-

---

[4]These measures of added years of life are adjusted for disability and are therefore known as disability-adjusted life-years (DALYs). The comparison is with the EPI Plus cluster of interventions—the Expanded Programme of Immunization plus hepatitis B and yellow fever vaccines and vitamin A and iodine supplements, where these micronutrients are deficient (World Bank, 1993b, p. 74, 84–85). For some commentary on these estimates, see Haaga et al. (1996).

ception and concern about its health effects, the two major reasons for the unmet need for contraception.

The majority of developing country governments do in fact take some responsibility for family planning, although their efforts have often been more notable at raising awareness levels than at ensuring quality services. Except in sub-Saharan Africa and scattered countries elsewhere, governments typically cover the bulk of publicly financed family planning expenditures in developing countries (Ross et al., 1993). The proportion of costs they cover tends to rise as programs develop: from under 30 percent to more than 60 percent of funding over the 1980s in Tunisia, for instance (Figure 16). But donor funds from industrial-country development assistance, international agencies, and private sources do fill critical gaps in funding.

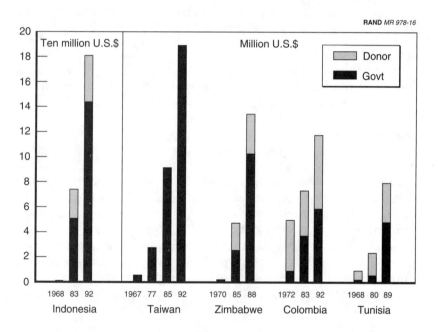

SOURCE: Donaldson and Tsui (1990, p. 27) and Ross et al. (1993, pp. 123–131).

Figure 16—Government and Donor Spending on Family Planning,
Selected Countries and Years

DONOR COMMITMENTS

International donors play an important role in getting programs started, and also later in helping them expand. Donor funding typically increases over time—although government funding generally rises much faster—as a program tries to reach a larger clientele and becomes more skilled and sophisticated in doing so. Donor funding usually declines when a program is fairly mature and well-established.

In several ways, donors find family planning programs ideal humanitarian programs. These programs benefit the poorest in society, those unable to afford such a basic service on their own, and they benefit women in particular. They provide households not only with a concrete service but also with the opportunity to better their lot and improve the prospects for their children. Programs now have a record of success in many countries, but still have a long way to go and require much further assistance in others. Besides their personal benefits for individuals and households, programs also open up opportunities for societal development through the reduced dependency burden. By releasing some pressure on resources, they allow societies the time and opportunity to develop more sustainable modes of interacting with their environments.

Family planning assistance is not comparable in its immediate commercial benefits to "foreign aid" programs that directly promote exports , but the benefits it does provide may be wider and longer lasting.[5] If developing countries can be assisted in achieving low population growth and progressive economies, the benefits to the donor countries of growing markets, increasing international division of labor, and expanded export and investment opportunities could be considerable. In the United States, the leading donor in this area, a third of economic growth in the past decade has been generated by exports (Bergsten, 1997), and strong economies overseas have been essential to this. The American "economic future is increasingly tied to growing foreign markets,"[6] as the stock market

---

[5]And they could be potentially greater, if the other programs involve significant trade diversion rather than trade creation.

[6]Joe Lockhart, in explaining Bill Clinton's foreign travel (*Wall Street Journal*, 15 Oct 1997).

gyrations in October 1997 demonstrated.   In addition, strong economies in developing countries promote political stability and facilitate cooperation on international problems, from drugs and crime to global warming to uncontrolled migration.[7]

In line with its activist foreign policy, the United States has been the leading international donor in population and family planning, with about half of all contributions and an overseas staff and technical advisers who constitute the bulk of such donor expertise in the field in developing countries. However, the U.S. share of contributions diminished in the late 1980s and has not recovered to previous levels. In fact, U.S. population assistance fell 20 percent from FY 1995 to FY 1996 and fell a further 10 percent in FY 1997.[8] How other donor countries will react to this is difficult to predict.

As the United States has become increasingly engaged with the rest of the world—through expanding trade and alliances; through international agreements on security assistance, drug enforcement, environmental protection, etc.; and through the growing band of American expatriates, whose numbers have risen by 50 percent in the 1990s[9]—its commitment to assisting needy countries appears to have actually diminished. The United States devotes less of its GNP to all official development assistance than any of the other 20 leading industrial economies. Per capita, U.S. official development assistance in all areas is equivalent to a contribution of US$0.70 per week from each American, as contrasted with US$2.00 from each Japanese and more than US$5.00 from each Dane and Norwegian.[10] U.S. assistance is declining at the same time that assistance from all

---

[7]A list of such arguments for tax-supported foreign aid is provided by Cohen (1997). Quantifying such benefits is largely a speculative exercise, but if one considers all foreign aid from all sources, the benefits in trade promoted, wars avoided, and environmental damage averted are reportedly thousands of times the cost of the assistance (O'Hanlon and Graham, 1997). With regard to migration, it is not being argued that reducing migration produces economic benefits. Within limits and with qualifications, the reverse appears to be the case (Smith and Edmonston, 1997). But a lawful, controlled process—though not necessarily a restrictive one—is desirable.

[8]Reported figures for these years are US$541.6 million, $432 million, and $385 million. For FY 1998, no change is expected.

[9]Excluding soldiers and diplomats (Knowlton, 1997).

[10]Estimates of official development assistance are for 1994 (World Bank, 1997a, p. 304) and are compared with the 1995 population.

OECD countries combined is also declining: by 6 percent from 1995 to 1996, leaving the OECD countries less than half way to their target of devoting 0.7 percent of their GNP to reducing world poverty (Randel and German, 1997).

Relative to other countries, the United States puts more of its development assistance into population—4 percent in 1993, 5 percent in 1994, and a reported 9 percent in 1995 (when reproductive health began to be counted by UNFPA [1997a], and all U.S. development assistance fell by one-fourth[11]). Even the sharply higher proportion in that single year, however, meant that support for population and reproductive health in developing countries costs each American only a penny a day.

These pennies have added up and made a difference, but the U.S. role has been much deeper than that of a program financier. Many of the ideas and initiatives that carried international family planning from a long-shot, almost desperate attempt to alleviate developing-country poverty to the levels of sophistication and success it enjoys in some countries found their inspiration in U.S. think tanks and universities and their implementation with the support and advice of American agencies. U.S. support for strong population policies has been ubiquitous, sometimes pushing governments farther than they have been ready to go. Subsequent technical assistance has helped build institutions in certain countries that can contribute in a lasting fashion. The commitment of the United States and other donor countries to human rights and democratic principles has also been important in ensuring the voluntary character of these programs wherever these donors have been involved.

CONTINUING CHALLENGES

Programs have already made a substantial contribution to welfare in developing countries. From 1960 to 1990, the number of young dependents (under age 15) per 100 developing-country workers fell from 75 to 60. If, as noted earlier, family planning programs have been responsible for about 40 percent of fertility decline (Bongaarts, forthcoming), they would be responsible for two-thirds of this

---

[11]According to OECD, net U.S. official development assistance fell from US$9.9 billion in 1994 to $7.4 billion in 1995, then recovered somewhat to $9.4 billion in 1996.

reduction (Figure 17).   An essentially similar conclusion can be drawn from overall dependency ratios, which include older dependents.[12] Family planning has already reduced the burdens on and provided substantial opportunities for households and individuals in many countries.

But family planning programs still have much to accomplish. Each worker must still provide for 10 to 15 percent more dependents than in industrial countries, with all this implies in poorer health and obstacles to development. These burdens are projected to decline, but such projections are contingent on continued program success— on the family planning movement remaining as strong and innovative into the next century as it has been in the last decades of this century. If programs somehow disintegrate, the reduction in young dependents will be only half what it might be by 2020 and only a

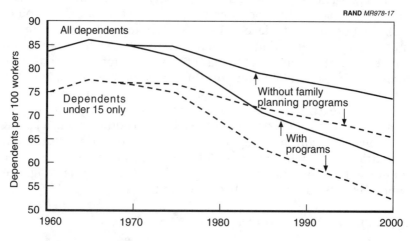

SOURCE: United Nations (1996) and projections using the World Bank (1997a) model.

Figure 17—Effect of Family Planning Programs on the Dependency Burden in Developing Countries, 1960–2000

[12]The argument is based on population projections over this period, separately for China and for all other developing countries, that assume that fertility decline is only 60 percent of that reported. Assumptions and methods follow World Bank (1997a).

fourth of what it might be by 2050 (Figure 18). If somehow all fertility decline—due not only to programs but also to socioeconomic advance—came to a halt, the dependency burden would soon begin to rise.[13]

The technical challenges for family planning programs have not all been solved. If each program has to capitalize on existing demand to reduce fertility—essential for success, as was argued earlier—each needs the skills to investigate this demand among individuals and households and to develop and implement indigenous responses. Programs also increasingly recognize the need to craft new approaches to reach young adults, say between the ages of 15 and 24. This group, a slightly larger proportion of the population in the 1980s and 1990s (Figure 19), will reach 900 million by the turn of the cen-

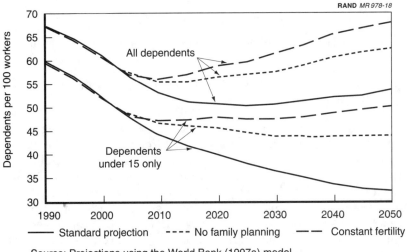

Source: Projections using the World Bank (1997a) model

**Figure 18—Projected Trends in Dependency in Developing Countries
Under Different Assumptions, 1990–2050**

---

[13]This is shown in population projections for China and for all other developing countries that assume, in one case, that fertility decline will be only 60 percent of the standard projection and, in another case, that fertility will remain constant. Assumptions and methods follow World Bank (1997a).

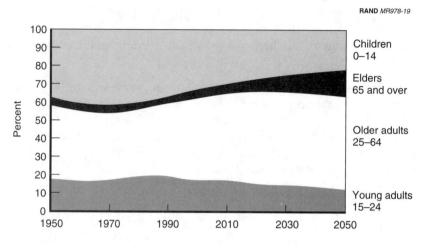

SOURCE: United Nations (1996) and projections using the World Bank (1997a) model.

Figure 19—Trends in Age Distribution in Developing Countries, 1950–2050

tury and will have considerable influence on the future trajectory of population growth.

As fertility declines, it becomes concentrated among young adults. As total fertility fell from 7.3 to 6.9 children per woman in Uganda from the mid-1980s to the early 1990s, the proportion of all births that were to women 15–24 rose from 46 to 52 percent. In India—where total fertility is much lower, at 3.4 children and where half of all young women are married before age 18—this proportion has reached 58 percent.[14]   Many pregnancies at these ages are not intended and would be postponed if possible, even among married women. The unmet need for contraception is increasing among young adults relative to its levels among older women. Figure 20 gives the ratios of unmet need in each age group to overall unmet

---

[14]Estimated from Uganda Demographic and Health Surveys (1988–1989 and 1995) and the India National Family Health Survey (1992–1993). An additional factor that exacerbates but does not entirely explain the Indian case has been the long failure to provide contraceptive methods useful for spacing births.

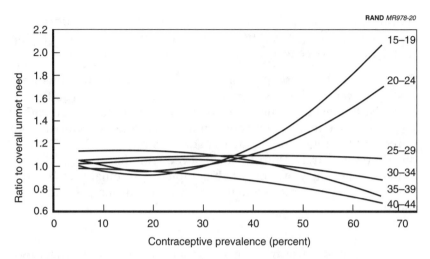

RAND *MR978-20*

SOURCE: Quadratic regressions estimated from data for 27 countries in Westoff and Bankole (1995, pp. 6, 9).

Figure 20—Ratio of Unmet Need in Each Age Group to Overall Unmet Need by Level of Contraceptive Prevalence

need, showing how these ratios are rising for young adults as overall contraceptive prevalence increases, even as they fall for older women.[15]

Much, though not all, of the need for contraception among young adults is for delaying or spacing births. With the realization that delaying births can help reduce fertility faster and further (Bongaarts 1994), programs face new challenges and a need to refurbish their goals and promotional approaches.[16] Programs also face additional challenges in improving service quality; dealing with sexually transmitted diseases, including HIV/AIDS; and ensuring broader attention to women's reproductive health needs, as the world com-

---

[15]The quadratic equations defining these curves were estimated across 27 countries with data (Westoff and Bankole, 1995, pp. 6, 9) that cover the range of contraceptive prevalence estimates in this graph. R^2 for the equation for age group 15–19 was 0.68 and for age group 20–24, 0.72, both significant.

[16]Any fertility reduction, whether or not due to birth delay, means that future population momentum will be less, or at least will not grow as much as it otherwise would.

munity called for at the Cairo conference. Assisting countries to meet such challenges will be difficult without American leadership and the continued engagement of American expertise.

Funds to assist developing-country family planning programs were first approved by the U.S. Congress three decades ago. The United States still provides almost half of all donor funding,[17] but other countries have increasingly contributed: Europe now provides 40 percent of the total, and Japan, Canada, Australia, and New Zealand all add their shares. With the task of reducing fertility and dependency around the world only half completed, it remains to be seen whether the United States and its allies will stay the course and finish the job.

---

[17]The reference is to "primary" donor funding in 1995, which includes funds passed through multilateral agencies and international nongovernmental organizations (UNFPA, 1997a).

REFERENCES

Ahlburg, Dennis A., "Population Growth and Poverty," in Dennis A. Ahlburg, Allen C. Kelley, and Karen Oppenheim Mason, eds., *The Impact of Population Growth on Well-Being in Developing Countries*, Berlin: Springer-Verlag, 1996, pp. 219–258.

Ahlburg, Dennis, and Eric Jensen, "Education and the East Asian Miracle," paper prepared for the Conference on Population and the Asian Economic Miracle, East-West Center, Honolulu, January 7–10, 1997.

Angeles, Gustavo, Thomas A. Mroz, and David K. Guilkey, "Purposive Program Placement and the Estimation of Program Effects: The Impact of Family Planning Programs in Tanzania," paper prepared for the annual meeting of the Population Association of America, April 6–8, San Francisco, 1995.

Bankole, Akinrinola, and Alfred A. Adewuyi, *Multi-Media Campaigns, Interpersonal Contacts and Contraceptive Behavior in Southwest Nigeria*, Chapel Hill, N.C.: EVALUATION Project, 1994.

Bankole, Akinrinola, and Charles F. Westoff, *Childbearing Attitudes and Intentions*, DHS Comparative Studies No. 17, Calverton, Md.: Macro International Inc., 1995.

Bankole, Akinrinola, Germán Rodríguez, and Charles F. Westoff, "The Mass Media and Reproductive Behavior in Nigeria," *Journal of Biosocial Science*, Vol. 23, No. 2, 1996, pp. 227–239.

Bauman, Karl E., "True Experimental Design for Family Planning Program Evaluation," EVALUATION Project final technical report, Chapel Hill, N.C.: University of North Carolina, 1994.

Berelson, Bernard, "National Family Planning Programs: A Guide," *Studies in Family Planning*, Vol. 1, No. 5 (Supplement), 1964, pp. 1–12.

Bergsten, C. Fred, "American Politics, Global Trade," *Economist*, September 27, 1997, pp. 23–26.

Bernhart, Michael H., "Management of Family Planning Programs and Operations Research," in Myrna Seidman and Marjorie C. Horn, eds., *Operations Research: Helping Family Planning Programs Work Better*, New York: Wiley-Liss, 1991, pp. 143–180.

Bertrand, Jane T., "Recent Lessons from Operations Research on Service Delivery Mechanisms," in Myrna Seidman and Marjorie C. Horn, eds., *Operations Research: Helping Family Planning Programs Work Better*, New York: Wiley-Liss, 1991, pp. 19–44.

Birdsall, Nancy, "Another Look at Population and Global Warming," in United Nations, *Population, Environment, and Development*, New York, 1994, pp. 39–54.

Bloom, David E., and Jeffrey G. Williamson, *Demographic Transitions and Economic Miracles in Emerging Asia*, National Bureau of Economic Research Working Paper No. 6268, 1997.

Bongaarts, John, "Population Policy Options in the Developing World," *Science*, Vol. 263, No. 5148, 1994, pp. 771–776.

_____, "The Role of Family Planning Programs in Contemporary Fertility Transitions," in G. W. Jones and J. Caldwell, eds., *The Continuing Demographic Transition*, London: Oxford University Press, forthcoming.

Bongaarts, John, and Judith Bruce, "The Causes of Unmet Need for Contraception and the Social Content of Services," *Studies in Family Planning*, Vol. 26, No. 2, 1995, pp. 57–75.

Bongaarts, John, and Susan Cotts Watkins, "Social Interactions and Contemporary Fertility Transitions," *Population and Development Review*, Vol. 22, No. 4, 1996, pp. 639–682.

Boone, M. S., J. U. Farley, and S. J. Samuel, "A Cross-Country Study of Commercial Contraceptive Sales Programs: Factors that Lead to Success," *Studies in Family Planning*, Vol. 16, No. 1, 1985, pp. 96–102.

Brown, Lisanne, Mostafa Tyane, Jane Bertrand, Don Lauro, Mohamed Abou-ouakil, and Lisa de Maria, "Quality of Care in Family Planning Services in Morocco," *Studies in Family Planning*, Vol. 26, No. 3, 1995, pp. 154–168.

Bulatao, Rodolfo A., *Expenditures on Population Programs in Developing Regions: Current Levels and Future Requirements*, Washington, D.C.: World Bank, World Bank Staff Working Paper No. 679, 1985.

_____, "Effectiveness and Evolution in Family Planning Programs," in *International Population Conference*, Vol. 1, Liege, Belgium: International Union for the Scientific Study of Population, 1993, pp. 189–200.

_____, *Evolving Dimensions of Family Planning Effort from 1982 to 1994*, report prepared for the Futures Groups International, Inc., Glastonbury, Conn., 1996.

Bulatao, Rodolfo A., and Ann Elwan, *Fertility and Mortality Transition: Patterns, Projections, and Interdependence*, Washington, D.C.: World Bank, World Bank Staff Working Paper No. 681, 1985.

Casterline, John B., Aurora E. Perez, and Ann E. Biddlecom, "Factors Underlying Unmet Need in the Philippines," *Studies in Family Planning*, Vol. 28, No. 3, 1997, pp. 173–191.

Cleland, John, James F. Phillips, Sajeda Amin, and G. M. Kamal, *The Determinants of Reproductive Change in Bangladesh: Success in a Challenging Environment*, Washington, D.C.: World Bank, 1994.

Cho, Lee-Jay, Fred Arnold, and Tai Hwan Kwon, *The Determinants of Fertility in the Republic of Korea*, Committee on Population and

Demography Report No. 14, Washington, D.C.: National Academy of Sciences, 1982.

Coale, Ansley, and Edgar Hoover, *Population Growth and Economic Development in Low-Income Countries*, Princeton, N.J.: Princeton University Press, 1958.

Cochrane, Susan H., *The Effects of Education, Health, and Social Security on Fertility in Developing Countries*, Policy, Planning, and Research Working Papers No. 93, Washington, D.C.: World Bank, 1988.

Cochrane, Susan H., and K. C. Zachariah, *Infant and Child Mortality as a Determinant of Fertility: The Policy Implications*, World Bank Staff Working Papers No. 556, Washington, D.C.: World Bank, 1983.

Cohen, Joel E., "Why Should More United States Tax Money Be Used to Pay for Development Assistance in Poor Countries?" *Population and Development Review*, Vol. 23, No. 3, 1997, pp. 579–584.

Cohen, Susan A., *The Role of Contraception in Reducing Abortion*, New York: Alan Guttmacher Institute, 1997.

Deaton, Angus S., and Christina H. Paxson, "The Effects of Economic and Population Growth on National Saving and Inequality," *Demography*, Vol. 34, No. 1, 1997, pp. 97–114.

Donaldson, Peter J., and Amy Ong Tsui, "The International Family Planning Movement," *Population Bulletin*, Vol. 45, No. 3, 1990.

Eloundou-Enyegue, Parfait M., Demographic Responses to Economic Crisis in Cameroon: Fertility, Child Schooling and the Quantity/Quality Tradeoff, Ph.D. dissertation, Pennsylvania State University, 1997.

Ezeh, Alex C., Michka Seroussi, and Hendrik Raggers, *Men's Fertility, Contraceptive Use, and Reproductive Preferences*, DHS Comparative Studies No. 18, Calverton, Md.: Macro International Inc., 1996.

Family Health International, *A Penny a Day*, Research Triangle Park, N.C., 1990.

Finkle, Jason L., and Gayl D. Ness, *Managing Delivery Systems—Identifying Leverage Points for Improving Family Planning Program Performance*, final report, Ann Arbor, Mich.: Department of Population Planning and International Health, University of Michigan, December 28, 1985.

Foreit, James R., and Karen G. Foreit, "Quarterly Versus Monthly Supervision of CBD Family Planning Programs: An Experimental Study in Northeast Brazil," *Studies in Family Planning*, Vol. 15, No. 3, 1984, pp. 112–120.

Foster, Andrew D., and Nikhil Roy, "The Dynamics of Education and Fertility: Evidence from a Family Planning Experiment," unpublished paper, Department of Economics, University of Pennsylvania, Philadelphia, 1993.

Freedman, Ronald, "Family Planning Programs in the Third World," *Annals of the American Academy of Political and Social Science*, Vol. 510, 1990, pp. 33–43.

Gallen, Moira E., and Ward Rinehart, *Operations Research: Lessons for Policy and Programs*, Population Reports, Series J, No. 31, 1986.

Haaga, John, Amy O. Tsui, and Judith Wasserheit, eds., *Reproductive Health Interventions: Report of a Meeting*, Washington, D.C.: National Academy Press, 1996.

Harrison, P. F., and A. Rosenfield, eds., *Contraceptive Research and Development: Looking to the Future*, Washington, D.C.: National Academy Press, 1996.

Higgins, Matthew, and Jeffrey G. Williamson, "Age Structure Dynamics in Asia and Dependence on Foreign Capital," *Population and Development Review*, Vol. 23, No. 2, 1997, pp. 261–293.

Huber, Sallie Craig, and Philip D. Harvey, "Family Planning Programmes in Ten Developing Countries: Cost Effectiveness by Mode of Service Delivery," *Journal of Biosocial Science*, Vol. 21, 1989, pp. 267–277.

Isaacs, Stephen L., "Incentives, Population Policy, and Reproductive Rights: Ethical Issues," *Studies in Family Planning*, Vol. 26, No. 6, 1995, pp. 363–367.

Ji, Liali, "China's One-Child Policy: A Case Study of Hebei Province, 1979–88," *Population and Development Review*, Vol. 21, No. 3, 1995, pp. 563–585.

Keller, Alan, Pierre Severyns, Atiqur Khan, and Nicholas Dodd, "Toward Family Planning in the 1990s: A Review and Assessment," *International Family Planning Perspectives*, Vol. 15, No. 4, 1989, pp. 127–135.

Kelley, Allen C., and Robert M. Schmidt, "Saving, Dependency and Development," *Journal of Population Economics*, Vol. 9, No. 4, 1996, pp. 365–386.

Knodel, John, Napaporn Havanon, and Werasit Sittitrai, "Family Size and the Education of Children in the Context of Rapid Fertility Decline," *Population and Development Review*, Vol. 16, No. 1, 1990, pp. 31–62.

Knowles, James C., "Cost-Benefit and Cost-Effectiveness Analysis in Family Planning," paper prepared for the Joint IUSSP/ EVALUATION Project Meeting on Methods for Evaluating Family Planning Programme Impact, Costa Rica, May 14–16, 1997.

Knowlton, Brian, "All Abroad! A Surge in Expatriate Americans," *International Herald Tribune*, October 13, 1997.

Krugman, Paul, *What Happened to Asia?* Cambridge, Mass.: Massachusetts Institute of Technology, 1998.

Lande, Robert E., and Judith S. Geller, *Paying for Family Planning*, Population Reports, Series J, No. 39, 1991.

Lee, Ronald, Andrew Mason, and Timothy Miller, "Saving, Wealth, and the Demographic Transition in East Asia," paper prepared for the Conference on Population and the Asian Economic Miracle, East-West Center, Honolulu, January 7–10, 1997.

Lewis, Maureen A., *Pricing and Cost Recovery Experience in Family Planning Programs*, World Bank Staff Working Papers No. 684, Washington, D.C., 1985.

_____, "Cost of Contraceptive Supplies and Services and Cost-Sharing, in United Nations," *Family Planning, Health and Family Well Being,* New York, 1996, pp. 256–274 .

Lloyd, Cynthia B., "Investing in the Next Generation: The Implications of High Fertility at the Level of the Family," in Cassen, Robert, and contributors, *Population and Development: Old Debates, New Conclusions,* New Brunswick: Transaction Publishers, 1994, pp. 181–202.

Maine, Deborah, *Safe Motherhood Programs: Options and Issues,* New York: Columbia University, Center for Population and Family Health, 1991.

Maine, Deborah, and Regina McNamara, *Birth Spacing and Child Survival,* New York: Columbia University, Center for Population and Family Health, 1985.

Mason, Andrew, "Population, Housing, and the Economy," in Dennis A. Ahlburg, Allen C. Kelley, and Karen Oppenheim Mason, eds., *The Impact of Population Growth on Well-Being in Developing Countries,* Berlin: Springer-Verlag, 1996, pp. 175–218.

Mazur, Laurie Ann, *High Stakes: The United States, Global Population and Our Common Future,* New York: The Rockefeller Foundation, 1997.

McNicoll, Geoffrey, *Fertility Decline in Indonesia: Analysis and Interpretation,* Committee on Population and Demography Report No. 20, Washington, D.C.: National Academy Press, 1983.

Montgomery, Mark R., and Cynthia B. Lloyd, "High Fertility, Unwanted Fertility and Children's Schooling," paper presented at the National Academy of Sciences Workshop on Education and Fertility in the Developing World, Washington, D.C., February–March 1996.

Montgomery, Mark R., Cynthia B. Lloyd, Paul C. Hewett, and Patrick Heuveline, *The Consequences of Imperfect Fertility Control for Children's Survival, Health and Schooling,* DHS Analytical Studies, Calverton, Md.: Macro International Inc., forthcoming.

Mukaire, Joy, Florence Kalikwani, Baker Ndugga Maggwa, and Wilson Kisubi, *Integration of STI and HIV/AIDS Services with MCH-FP Services: A Case Study of the Busoga Diocese Family Life Education Program, Uganda*, Nairobi: Operations Research Technical Assistance, Africa Project II, Population Council, 1997.

Ness, Gayl D., and Hirofumi Ando, *The Land Is Shrinking: Population Planning in Asia*, Baltimore, Md.: Johns Hopkins University Press, 1984.

Ness, Gayl D., P. Hemrajani, S. Bernstein, and J. T. Johnson, *Population Policy: A Major Third World Revolution*, Program Determinants Project Working Paper No. 5, Ann Arbor, Mich.: University of Michigan, Center for Population Planning, 1983.

Nortman, Dorothy L., and Joanne Fisher, *Population and Family Planning Programs: A Compendium of Data Through 1981*, 11th ed., New York: Population Council, 1982.

O'Hanlon, Michael, and Carol Graham, *A Half Penny on the Federal Dollar: The Future of Development Aid*, Washington, D.C.: Brookings Institution, 1997.

Page, John, et al., *The East Asian Miracle: Economic Growth and Public Policy*, New York: Oxford University Press, 1993.

Palloni, Alberto, "The Relation Between Population and Deforestation: Methods for Drawing Causal Inferences from Macro and Micro Studies," in L. Arizpe, M. P. Stone, and D. C. Major, eds., *Population and Environment: Rethinking the Debate*, Boulder, Colo.: Westview Press, 1994, pp. 125–165.

Panayotou, Theodore, "The Population, Environment, and Development Nexus," in Robert Cassen and contributors, *Population and Development: Old Debates, New Conclusions*, New Brunswick: Transaction Publishers, 1994, pp. 149–180.

Paul, Samuel, "The Strategic Management of Development Programmes: Evidence from an International Study," *International Review of Administrative Sciences*, Vol. 1, 1983, pp. 73–86.

Phillips, James F., Emily Zimmerman, and Jiali Li, "Estimating the Demographic Impact of Family Planning Programs in Six

Developing Countries with DHS Accessiblity Data," paper prepared for the annual meeting of the Population Association of America, Cincinnati, Ohio, April 1–3, 1994.

Population Action International, *Why Population Matters*, Washington, D.C., 1996.

Preston, Samuel H., "The Effect of Population Growth on Environmental Quality: A Brief Assessment," paper presented under the auspices of the International Union for the Scientific Study of Population at the NGO Conference at the International Conference on Population and Development, Cairo, Egypt, September 5–12, 1994.

Pritchett, Lant H., "Desired Fertility and the Impact of Population Policies," *Population and Development Review*, Vol. 20, No. 1, 1994a, pp. 1–55.

_____, "The Impact of Population Policies: Reply," *Population and Development Review*, Vol. 20, No. 3, 1994b, pp. 621–630.

Ramesh, B. M., S. C. Gulati, and R. D. Retherford, *Contraceptive Use in India, 1992–1993*, National Family Health Survey Subject Reports No. 2, Mumbai: International Institute for Population Sciences, and Honolulu: East-West Center Program on Population, 1996.

Randel, Judith, and Tony German, eds., *The Reality of Aid 1997/98*, London: Earthscan Publications Ltd., 1997.

Robey, Bryant, John Ross, and Indra Bhushan, *Meeting Unmet Need: New Strategies*, Population Reports, Series J, No. 43, 1996.

Rosenzweig, Mark R., and Kenneth I. Wolpin, "Testing the Quantity-Quality Fertility Model: The Use of Twins as a Natural Experiment," *Econometrica*, Vol. 48, No. 1, 1980, pp. 227–240.

Ross, John, "The Question of Access," *Studies in Family Planning*, Vol. 26, No. 4, 1995, pp. 241–242.

Ross, John, and Elizabeth Frankenberg, *Findings from Two Decades of Family Planning Research*, New York: Population Council, 1993.

Ross, John A., W. Parker Mauldin, and Vincent C. Miller, *Family Planning and Population: A Compendium of International Statistics*, New York: Population Council, 1993.

Rutstein, Shea O., *Infant and Child Mortality: Levels, Trends and Demographic Differentials*, Comparative Studies, No. 24, London: World Fertility Survey, 1983.

Samara, Renee, Bates Buckner, and Amy Ong Tsui, *Understanding How Family Planning Programs Work: Findings from Five Years of Evaluation Research*, Chapel Hill, N.C.: EVALUATION Project, Carolina Population Center, University of North Carolina, 1996.

Schultz, T. Paul, "School Expenditures and Enrollments, 1960–80: The Effects of Income, Prices, and Population Growth," in D. Gale Johnson, and Ronald D. Lee, eds., *Population Growth and Economic Development: Issues and Evidence*, Madison, Wisc.: University of Wisconsin Press, 1987, pp. 413–476.

Simmons, George B., Deborah Balk, and Khodezatul K. Faiz, "Cost-Effectiveness Analysis of Family Planning Programs in Rural Bangladesh: Evidence from Matlab," *Studies in Family Planning*, Vol. 22, No. 2, 1991, pp. 83–101.

Simmons, Ruth, "Supervision: The Management of Front-Line Performance," in Robert J. Lapham and George B. Simmons, eds., *Organizing for Effective Family Planning Programs*, Washington, D.C.: National Academy Press,1987, pp. 233–262.

Simon, Julian L., *The Ultimate Resource*, Princeton, N.J.: Princeton University Press, 1981.

Smith, James P., and Barry Edmonston, eds., *The New Americans: Economic, Demographic, and Fiscal Aspects of Immigration*, Washington, D.C.: National Academy Press, 1997.

Snow, Rachel, Sandra Garcia, Nazo Kureshy, Ritu Sadana, Sagri Singh, Mercedes Becerra-Valdivia, Star Lancaster, Mamorena Mofokeng, Margaret Hoffman, and Iain Aitken, *Investigating Women's Preferences for Attributes of Contraceptive Technology: Focus Group Data from Seven Countries*, Geneva: World Health Organization Human Reproduction Programme, n.d.

Sullivan, Jeremiah M., Shea Oscar Rutstein, and George T. Bicego, *Infant and Child Mortality*, DHS Comparative Studies, No. 15, Calverton, Md.: Macro International Inc., 1994.

Summers, Robert, Alan Heston, Bettina Aten, and Daniel A. Nuxoll, *Penn World Tables*, Mark 5.6a, Philadelphia: Center for International Comparison, University of Pennsylvania, 1995. (Cited in Andrew Mason, *Population and the Asian Economic Miracle*, Asia-Pacific Population Policy No. 43, Honolulu: East-West Center, Program on Population, 1997.)

Tamayo, Fernando, "Profamilia: A Case Study of Strategic Planning and Management," in Gayl Ness and Ellen Sattar, eds., *Strategic Management of Population Programmes*, Kuala Lumpur: ICOMP, 1989, pp. 152–186.

Townsend, John W., "Effective Family Planning Service Components: Global Lessons from Operations Research," in Myrna Seidman and Marjorie C. Horn, eds., *Operations Research: Helping Family Planning Programs Work Better*, New York: Wiley-Liss, 1991, pp. 45–96 .

Tsui, Amy Ong, "Population Policies and Programs and the Asian Economic Miracle," paper prepared for the annual meeting of the Population Association of America, Washington, D.C., March 27–29, 1997.

Tsui, Amy Ong, and Luis Hernando Ochoa, "Service Proximity as a Determinant of Contraceptive Behavior: Evidence from Cross-National Studies of Survey Data," in James F. Phillips and John A. Ross, eds., *Family Planning Programmes and Fertility*, Oxford.: Clarendon Press, 1989, pp. 222–256.

Tsui, Amy Ong, Judith N. Wasserheit, and John G. Haaga, eds., *Reproductive Health in Developing Countries: Expanding Dimensions, Building Solutions*, Washington, D.C.: National Academy Press, 1997.

Twahir, Amina, Baker Ndugga Maggwa, and Ian Askew, *Integration of STI and HIV/AIDS Services with MCH-FP Services: A Case Study of the Mkomani Clinic Society in Mombasa, Kenya*, Nairobi: Operations Research Technical Assistance, Africa Project II, Population Council, 1996.

United Nations, Department for Economic and Social Information and Policy Analysis, Population Division, *World Population Prospects: The 1996 Revision*, New York, 1996.

United Nations Population Fund (UNFPA), *Family Planning Logistics Systems: The Situation in 18 African Countries*, New York, 1990.

_____, *Global Population Assistance Report 1982–1990*, New York, 1992.

_____, *Background Note on the Resource Requirements for Population Programmes in the Years 2000–2015*, New York, July 13, 1994.

_____, *Global Population Assistance Report 1993*, New York, 1995.

_____, *Global Population Assistance Report 1995*, New York, 1997a.

_____, *Meeting the Goals of the ICPD: Consequences of Resource Shortfalls up to the Year 2000*, New York, 1997b.

Vriesendorp, Sylvia, Laurel K. Cobb, Saul Helfenbein, Judith A. Levine, and James Wolff, Jr., "A Framework for Management Development of Family Planning Program Managers," paper presented at the Annual Meeting of the American Public Health Association, Chicago, Ill., October 24, 1989.

Warwick, Donald P., *Bitter Pills*, Cambridge, England: Cambridge University Press, 1982.

Westoff, Charles F., and Akinrinola Bankole, *Unmet Need: 1990–1994*, DHS Comparative Studies No. 16, Calverton, Md.: Macro International Inc., 1995.

Westoff, Charles F., Germán Rodríguez, and Akinrinola Bankole, *Family Planning and Mass Media Messages*, Chapel Hill, N.C.: EVALUATION Project, 1994.

Williamson, Jeffrey G., and Matthew Higgins, "The Accumulation and Demography Connection in East Asia," paper prepared for the Conference on Population and the Asian Economic Miracle, East-West Center, Honolulu, January 7–10, 1997.

World Health Organization, "User Preferences for Contraceptive Methods in India, Korea, the Philippines, and Turkey," *Studies in Family Planning,* Vol. 11, No. 9/10, 1980, pp. 267–273.

World Bank, *Effective Family Planning Programs,* Washington, D.C., 1993a.

_____, *World Development Report 1993,* Washington, D.C., 1993b.

_____, *World Development Report 1996,* Washington, D.C., 1996.

_____, *World Development Indicators,* Washington, D.C., 1997a.

_____, *World Development Report 1997,* Washington, D.C., 1997b.